# Dales
# Tea Shop Walks

*in the*

## PEAK DISTRICT

*Andrew McCloy*

*25 scenic walks including
traditional tea shops*

# Dalesman

Dalesman Publishing Company
Stable Courtyard, Broughton Hall,
Skipton, North Yorkshire BD23 3AZ


First Edition 1999


Text © Andrew McCloy, 1999
Illustrations © Donald Dakeyne
Maps by Jeremy Ashcroft


Cover: Meadow Cottage Tea Garden, Youlgreave, by
Geoff Cowton


A British Library Cataloguing in Publication record
is available for this book

ISBN 1 85568 142 0

Printed by Midas Printing (HK) Ltd

# Dalesman's
# Tea Shop Walks

### *in the*
## *PEAK DISTRICT*

*Andrew McCloy*

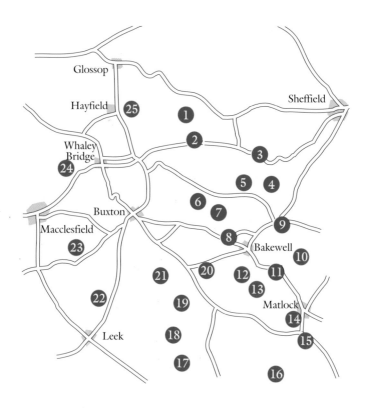

# WALKS

*This book is dedicated to my brother, Paul McCloy,
a devotee of high places*

# INTRODUCTION

There's a lot to be said for taking regular countryside walks: they're healthy and relaxing, allow you to pursue a conversation or your own thoughts in depth, and getting away from everyday bustle lets you recharge the batteries and usually see some wildlife. But, for me, the overriding benefit of a good old ramble is that afterwards you can walk into a tea room and order the largest slice of cake in sight without the slightest shred of guilt. Quite simply, you will have deserved it.

When I was a little younger I imagined the thirst of a long walk could only be slaked by beer; but while this still has its place at the very end of the day there is nothing better than a hot, steaming cuppa immediately after you sit down and loosen the boot laces. It's cheaper but equally refreshing, there are no side-effects, and you don't have to venture into some smoky old pub to find it. And, of course, tea shops come in all shapes and sizes. I have selected a range of establishments from across the Peak District, each one dedicated to satisfying your appetite with a tasty brew and some mouth-watering, home-made delicacies. There are many family-run cottage tea rooms, where you can almost see granny in the kitchen rolling out the oatcakes; then there are others like the splendid Grindleford Station Cafe where tea comes in pint mugs and the chip butties would block a motorway.

Above all else, these 25 tea shop walks enable you to explore the varied and beautiful scenery of the Peak District: from high, wild moors to delectable limestone valleys rich in wildlife, plus old packhorse routes and former railway lines now converted into safe and enjoyable walking routes.

Have a great time.

*Andrew McCloy*

# DALE COTTAGE CAFE

EDALE

*A n easy walk around the unspoilt head of Edale connecting old farming settlements*

TEA SHOP:
Dale Cottage
Cafe, by Edale
Station
OPEN: Daily,
Mar-Oct;
weekends only,
Nov-Feb
MAP: OS
Outdoor Leisure 1
DISTANCE: 4
miles (6.5 km)
ALLOW: 2
hours
PARKING:
Large public car
park at Edale

The head of the Edale valley is dotted with a series of small settlements that share a common name: Barber Booth, Upper Booth, Nether Booth, Ollerbrook Booth and Grindsbrook Booth (the last is in fact the correct name for the collection of buildings centred on the Old Nags Head pub, usually referred to as Edale). The term 'booth' basically means a simple hut or shelter for a herdsman and his animals, since these tiny places all originated as early farming settlements. In addition, trains of packhorses regularly came through Edale on their long journey across the southern Pennines, and the packhorse men (whose leaders were known as 'jaggers') would no doubt stop at the Old Nags Head for refreshment — in much the same way as do today's walkers.

From the large car park by the turning from the Hope road (which runs the length of the valley) go up this lane past the cafe and under the railway bridge, then on past the

Peak National Park Visitor Centre, which is well worth a visit, until you reach the Old Nags Head. This famous, 16th century pub marks the beginning of the Pennine Way, and is the popular starting point for many a long and adventurous day walk over the vast moorland table of Kinder Scout. If you have a little spare time after your own walk today you may like to continue along the lane beyond the pub for the path on the right that explores the lower reaches of Grindsbrook Clough, an impressive and dramatic valley that cuts into the southern flank of Kinder Scout.

Turn left (opposite the pub) for a path indicated Upper

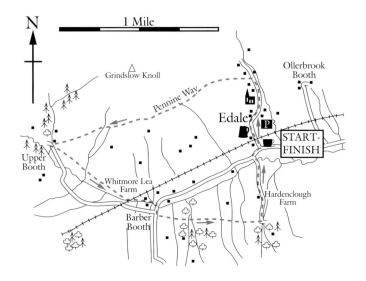

Booth/Pennine Way, and go through a kissing gate and on past farm buildings for a sunken path beneath a lengthy tunnel of holly trees alongside a brook. This was once known as Peat Lane, since it was used by villagers bringing peat turves down from the moors to burn as fuel in winter.

*You will already have noticed a few acorn signs which is the waymark for the Pennine Way National Trail. The first official long-distance footpath in Britain, it was devised by the late Tom Stephenson, long-time Secretary of the Ramblers' Association, who as far back as the 1930s envisaged a "long, green trail" that would stretch the length of England's backbone. The Pennine Way was officially opened in 1965, and connects the Peak District with the Scottish Borders, a distance of 256 miles (412 km), via the likes of the Yorkshire*

*Dales, Hadrian's Wall and Cheviot Hills. It offers invigorating but challenging walking, and none more so than the first stage across the featureless peat bogs of Kinder Scout and Bleaklow. If you want to explore the Pennine Way in detail make sure you are fit, well-equipped and familiar with a map and compass.*

At the end of the holly tunnel go left, over a stile, for an obvious and easy path across the lower slopes of the hillside. The first couple of miles of the Pennine Way — which you will walk today — are scenic and very straightforward, and the intermittently paved route across successive fields affords good views over the narrow valley towards Hollins Clough, Mam Tor and Rushup Edge.

After about a mile the track begins a steady descent to the hamlet of Upper Booth. Beyond this the Pennine Way pulls up its sleeves and prepares to climb Jacob's Ladder on to the high plateau, but your route is a little more sedate. As you turn left down a gravel drive and approach the farmyard, go left through a gate opposite sheep pens and ahead through a wide field. Go over a stile and veer half-right and then alongside a fence, first on your left then after another stile it's on your right. Follow occasional yellow waymarks through more fields until finally you join a clear farm track that makes its way over to the Manchester-Sheffield railway and swings left to cross it by a bridge.

Continue along the farm track, passing to the right of Whitmore Lea Farm. After this keep left and go past the small Methodist Chapel until the end of the small lane. Turn right and in a few yards you join the main road, and immediately after crossing the bridge above the river turn off left for a path signposted Castleton and Hope.

*In case you're wondering, the initials 'PD&NCFPS' on the sign stand for the Peak District and Northern Counties Footpaths Preservation Society, which was founded in 1894 and today maintains over 220 signposts to public rights of way in the region.*

You now climb very gently up the southern side of the valley, maintaining your direction through a succession of wide fields. Some are separated by small, wooded ravines known as 'cloughs', occasionally necessitating steps. Finally you come to Harden Clough, where you descend to a cool and shady lane. Turn left and follow this all the way down to the road at the bottom, where you turn right and then left to reach the cafe.

# CRYER HOUSE

*An exhilarating tour around the head of the Hope valley, via the high and panoramic summit of Mam Tor*

TEA SHOP:
Cryer House,
Castle Street,
Castleton
Tel 01433
620244
OPEN: Daily,
May–Sept;
weekends all
year
MAP: OS
Outdoor Leisure 1
DISTANCE:
5 miles (8 km)
ALLOW: 3
hours
PARKING:
Public car park
in centre of
Castleton

A walk in the Castleton area is inevitably steeped in history: from the Iron Age hillfort that once crowned the summit of the mighty Mam Tor, to the remains of Peveril Castle, a Norman stronghold established by the son of William the Conqueror and which gave its name to the village. Many come to Castleton for what lies underground. There are four popular caverns, offering the likes of subterranean boat rides (Speedwell), stalactites (Treak Cliff) and a cave entrance so huge that it was once used for rope-making (Peak). The fourth, Blue John Cavern, takes its name from the famous purple mineral mined here; but do bear in mind that if you plan to include a visit to any of the caverns allow plenty of extra time.

Go across the mini roundabout at the car park entrance and walk up the narrow lane opposite, indicated Peak Cavern, next to the stream. At the junction at the top turn right over the bridge and walk up Goosehill past some cottages, and as you do so you glimpse the spectacular entrance of Peak Cavern (60ft high and 100ft wide). Go through the gate at the end which leads into open pasture; then follow the path alongside the wall all the way around the head of the valley, with the steep slopes above.

When you finally arrive at the road next to Speedwell Cavern take a quick glance up at Winnats Pass and cross over to enter the rough field opposite for a path that continues past the cavern buildings (head for the small patch of woodland on the far side). The path goes around the left-hand side of the trees and on to join the surfaced path up to Treak Cliff Cavern entrance. Follow the signs for the public footpath around the back of the buildings and up and around the open hillside.

*Ahead is the impressive bulk of Mam Tor, the so-called Shivering Mountain since its unstable shale composition makes it prone to subsidence and landslips. The most notable victim of this is the A625 that used to snake its way around the lower slopes but is now closed for good following a dramatic landslide in 1977. From this excellent vantage point you can see exactly where the road used to run.*

Go over a stile and along the broad grassy track to Blue John Cavern. The path continues up and across the rough pasture beyond, and when you eventually reach a long cross-wall before Winnats Head Farm turn right and go over a stile in the corner of the field. Carry straight on across the next, then cross a road, and on the far side of the wall fork right. The grassy track across the National Trust's Windy Knoll joins another, then takes

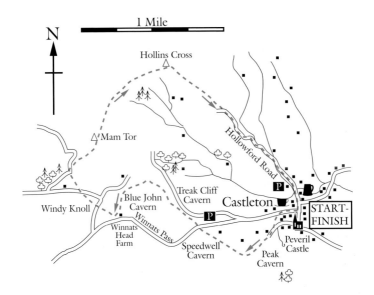

you across a road and up the slopes of Mam Tor. Follow
the signs at the gate by the road half way up, and ascend
the carefully flagged steps to the top.

*Assuming it's a clear day the views from the 1,695ft summit
are stupendous. The dark ridge of Kinder Scout and the lush
Edale valley below dominate the scenery to the north, while
the ridge ahead rises and falls to Lose Hill; beyond is the
volcanic cone of Win Hill. Immediately below you, on the far
side of the valley, the tiny cluster of Castleton nestles at the
foot of the ruined Peveril Castle, while further down the
valley the cement works near Bradwell is all too visible.*

After you have soaked up the views and run out of camera
film continue along the wide ridge track to Hollins Cross,
the low-point on the ridge where the paths from

# CRYER HOUSE

## C A S T L E T O N

Castleton and Edale meet. Turn half-right (not the path
sharply back to the foot of Mam Tor) and walk the initially
eroded track down towards Castleton. Beyond a gate this
develops into a sunken path, then after joining a farm lane
becomes the little-used Hollowford Road that leads all the
way back into the centre of Castleton. When you reach the
main road turn right and as you approach the car park
turn left by the Castle Inn. A few yards up on the right,
opposite the parish church, is Cryer House, where a pot of
tea and some very agreeable home baking will refresh even
the tiredest limbs.

Depending on your energy reserves, the steep zig-zag path up to Peveril Castle is approached further along Castle Street — continue beyond the tea rooms to the youth hostel and follow the signs.

*William the Conqueror made his illegitimate son, William Peveril, Steward of the Royal Forest of the Peak, and the eminently defendable Castleton site soon became an important Norman stronghold and one of the first stone-built castles in England. It was later added to by Henry II, and from its walls the superb views over the valley reveal in particular the grid-iron layout of Castleton's early street plan.*

# LONGLANDS EATING HOUSE

HATHERSAGE

*An energetic walk up to and along the high rocky vantage point of Stanage Edge, plus some curious connections with Robin Hood*

TEA SHOP:
Longlands Eating
House,
Hathersage
Tel 01433
651978
OPEN: Daily,
all year
MAP: OS
Outdoor Leisure 1
DISTANCE:
5 1/2 miles (9 km)
ALLOW: 3-4
hours
PARKING:
Public car park off
Grindleford road
at Hathersage

Longland's Eating House is to be found upstairs in the popular outdoor shop Outside, on the main street in Hathersage. Although it is run independently from the shop the opening hours of both the cafe and shop are similar, and most of the customers are walkers and climbers. The surroundings are comfortable and the food is wholesome and tasty; and after an afternoon on the windy heights of Stanage Edge what better place to relax and refresh yourself?

From the shop cross over and head up the main street and beyond the post office take the passageway directly behind the bank. At the top turn left into Baulk Lane, then shortly go right for an enclosed path up to the churchyard of St Michaels and All Angels.

*Opposite the door of the church you will see what is reputed to be the 10 feet-long grave of Little John, "friend and lieutenant of Robin Hood" as the modern gravestone puts it, who once lived in the village and is supposed to have died in a nearby cottage. In the porch of the church is what is said to be the original gravestone, bearing the initials 'J.L.' (John Little, perhaps?). The eastern Peak was once on the fringe of old Sherwood Forest, so that local connections with Robin Hood are not uncommon — later in the walk you will pass above Robin Hood's Cave on Stanage Edge.*

Proceed past the church entrance and turn right out of the lych gate, then walk down the drive and turn sharply left for a narrow lane that winds its way up among houses before heading more directly between fields. Follow this for almost half a mile to Carr Head Farm, then just past the buildings turn right for a faint grassy path up the bracken-covered bank above. The public footpath

continues directly through the sloping pasture in the wide field beyond. There is no defined path as such, so just head straight uphill with Carr Head behind you and you will soon arrive at or near the wall stile and signpost by the lane at the top. (A longer alternative to this steepish field crossing is to continue along the lane past Carr Head as it loops around via Kimber Court Farm and Leveret Croft).

Turn right on to the level lane and follow this to the end where you meet a road. Turn left and walk the grassy verge with widening views of Stanage Edge. When you come to a road junction, invariably surrounded by climbers' parked cars and minibuses, go diagonally ahead left for a well-walked track up towards the impressive gritstone edges above. Nearing the rocks take the right fork up on to the very top, and turn left for the popular track that runs the length of Stanage Edge.

*Stanage Edge is synonymous with climbing and climbers. On a popular weekend there will usually be hundreds of men and women swarming over the rocks, many having made the relatively short journey across the moors from Sheffield (a city which spawned many of the pioneers of British climbing). The 4-5 miles of continuous gritstone cliffs that make up Stanage Edge contain almost 1,000 separate climbing routes, with names like Heaven's Crack and The Unconquerable. Needless to say the drops are severe and there are a few unexpected cracks and crevices towards the edge, so make sure younger walkers take special care.*

The views from Stanage Edge are of course superb, especially of the Hope Valley and the dark outline of

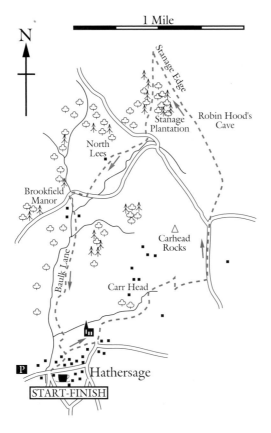

Kinder Scout and Bleaklow to the north. Meanwhile, on a rocky ledge immediately below you is Robin Hood's Cave, which considering that the legendary folk hero's birthplace, Loxley, is actually only six miles away in modern-day Sheffield, makes the association perhaps not so tenuous. At the foot of the edge is a small plantation, and as soon as you have passed this look out for a clear, semi-paved track that zig-zags down to the trees below. This former packhorse route — which accounts for the direct and well-made surface — heads diagonally down through the plantation and affords good views of the climbers tackling the rock faces above.

When you emerge on to open ground above the car park take the left of three tracks, and cross the road at the bottom for a short path that heads down left through the trees behind the toilet block. Then turn right when you meet a wide track, which soon leaves the woodland and proceeds down through a field and around to the left of the castellated ramparts of North Lees. This old manor house was thought to have been used as the model for Thornfield Hall in Charlotte Brontë's novel *Jane Eyre*, following her three-week stay at Hathersage Vicarage in 1845 (an anagram of North is Thorn, and Lees means a field!). Go down its driveway and at the road at the bottom turn right. Just before the bridge turn left for a clear track around Brookfield Manor. This continues as a well-walked path across the middle of a field where it joins a more distinctive farm track. Beyond some houses this becomes Baulk Lane and returns you to the centre of Hathersage.

# STATION CAFE

*An ascent to a moorland estate, then back down a dramatic and quite rocky wooded gorge*

TEA SHOP:
The Station
Cafe,
Grindleford
Tel 01433
631011
OPEN: Daily,
all year
MAP: OS
Outdoor Leisure
1 & 24
Distance: 3 ³/₄
miles (6 km)
ALLOW: 2-3
hours
PARKING:
Grindleford
Station
approach

The cafe at the former Grindleford Station is a deserved favourite among walkers and climbers in this part of the Peak District. The tea comes in pint mugs and the meals are large and filling. In fact the cafe even produces its own bottled spring water, since the nearby spring has been tapped for the benefit of the local community since 1898, and Grindleford Natural Spring Water is now an ongoing commercial concern. As the sign by the door puts it: "Climber, cyclist, runner, to all, come in and have a brew, but the day is long and not yet through, so take along some natural too..."

Go up the surfaced steps on the right-hand side of the cafe which takes you up to the main road above. Go left for a few yards and cross carefully in order to resume the initially steep path through Oaks Wood. Keep right at a fork, so that the small, rocky stream is

immediately to your right. As you approach a gate
ignore a sign indicating a footpath to the right and go
through the gate and continue uphill and gradually out
into the open.

When you finally clear the tree-line take the path across
the stream to the right that runs parallel to the wall
above the plantation. Where this wall turns abruptly
right you should turn left, and walk up a somewhat
indistinct path across the open but untidy hillside
towards a solitary silver birch. Maintain your general
direction until eventually you join a narrow, paved path
that heads towards the strip of dark woodland on the far
side. If you are in any doubt, keep the transmitter mast
on Eyam Moor, across the Derwent valley, directly
behind you.

At the far side go over steps in the wall and turn left to
join a wide and level woodland drive through the
Longshaw Estate. Go through a gate and ignoring any
cross paths follow this easy and delightful route via
wooded and open ground for a mile, enjoying great
views across the upper Derwent to the moors beyond,
until you reach a white gate by some fenced-off
rhododendron bushes. Go through the double pedestrian
gates on the left and along the path below Longshaw
Lodge to reach the National Trust information centre
and cafe. This is the perfect place for a mid-walk rest,
and maybe an ice cream or the like since it's all downhill
from here on!

*Longshaw Lodge was originally a shooting lodge for the Duke
of Rutland, and although it now consists of private flats the
National Trust runs the 1,600 acres of the Longshaw Estate.*

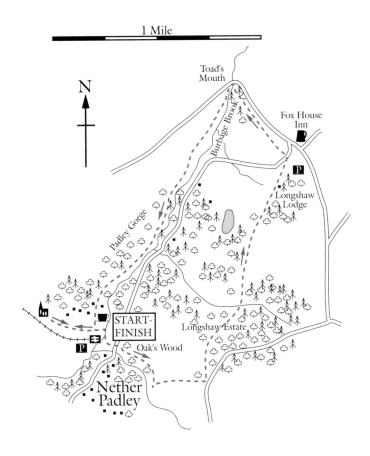

*Directly below the lodge is Longshaw Meadow where each September sheepdog trials take place. Among the oldest in the country, they started here in 1898 following an argument between farmers and shepherds in the nearby Fox House Inn over who owned the best sheepdog. Mind you, a century ago as*

*many as 9,000 sheep were driven up on to Longshaw Moors each year for winter pasturing.*

Continue along the drive and out of the gate to cross the road on the bend by the bus stop. Go through the gate on the far side and carry on down the wide track through more of the National Trust's estate, ignoring a turning on the right, until you descend to cross Burbage Brook by a wooden footbridge. On the far bank turn left and follow the well-used track downstream. On a summer's weekend this open, grassy strip is a popular venue for picnics; but before long the track enters woodland and the easy flowing brook tumbles down the wild and rocky Padley Gorge.

The wide, often rocky track sticks high above the noisy water, and winds its way through a dense covering of oak, home to a variety of birdlife including pied flycatchers and warblers. Ignore several smaller paths off to the right and keep to the main track, nearly always in sound if not in sight of the torrent far below on your left. At one point, by a large beech tree, an inviting path descends the gorge, but you should continue half-right on a rising track that soon resumes its gradual descent down the valley. This stone-pitched route soon emerges from the trees, and on the far side of a gate becomes a rough lane that drops down past houses.

*At the bottom you can turn right for a short diversion to visit Padley Chapel where, in the Armada year of 1588 and on a wave of anti-Catholic sentiment, two Roman Catholic priests were discovered hiding and arrested. Nicholas Garlick and Robert Ludlam were then taken to Derby where they were hanged, drawn and quartered. An annual pilgrimage honouring their memory takes place here each summer, and such is the interest in their martyrdom that in 1987 Pope John Paul II allowed the two priests to be called "Blessed".*

Otherwise turn left and follow the lane back to the cafe via the railway bridge, from where you have a close-up view of the trains entering Totley Tunnel, built in 1893 and at 6,230 yards one of the longest railway tunnels in Britain.

# EYAM TEA ROOMS

*This short but engrossing tour of the so-called plague village includes a wander up to the scenic ridge above*

TEA SHOP:
Eyam Tea
Rooms, The
Square, Eyam
Tel 01433
631274
OPEN: Daily
except Mon,
Easter-Oct;
weekends only
in Nov
MAP: OS
Outdoor Leisure 24
DISTANCE:
3 ¹/₂ miles
(5.5 km)
ALLOW: 2
hours
PARKING:
Public car park
opposite Eyam
Museum

Eyam (pronounced 'Eem') is an attractive village with a macabre history. In 1665 the Black Death was unknowingly introduced to this small community; but rather than flee and spread the disease the villagers decided to shut themselves off from outside contact and try to contain it — whatever the inevitably fatal consequences. Today you can walk around Eyam and trace the tragic story for yourself, since many of the older buildings bear plaques telling the fate of the inhabitants — for, within months, almost 260 or five out of every six had died.

Opposite the car park is Eyam Museum (open Tues-Sun, Mar-Nov), and your first decision will be whether to visit this now or when you finish the walk later on. It's probably more beneficial to go in at the start so that you will be more enlightened for the walk ahead, but there again you might also spend so long inside that it

will already be tea time when you emerge. Lucky it's only a short walk.

Turn right out of the car park and follow the lane uphill. Where it bends sharply right go half left up an unclassified road known as The Nook past several houses, and where they end carry on along a narrower track that climbs steadily uphill. This is the only ascent of the walk, but although it is not exceptionally steep it is unremitting, so take a breather and study the occasional views back over Eyam, and to the deep quarries of Stoney Middleton beyond.

At the top turn right along a lane, and in just under 300 yards look for steps in the wall on the left (a signposted public footpath is also visible just ahead off the lane to the right). The path leads up the right-hand edge of the field and continues to stick close to the wall through successive fields. Ahead and over the hill on your left is a transmitter mast, visible for miles around, while across the wall on your right is the chimney of the former Ladywash Mine which yielded lead and subsequently barytes and fluorspar.

At the end of the last field go over the wall and turn right into Sir William Hill Road. This wide, unsurfaced track divides the pasture from the wild moorland, and from this elevated position there are great views across the Derwent valley. When you arrive at the bend of a surfaced road turn right, and the sharp gritstone rim of Froggatt and Curbar Edges are even more apparent. Keep straight on until the road dips down to a junction, and just before this on the right make sure to visit Mompesson's Well.

*When the village was in its strict, self-imposed quarantine virtually all contact with the outside world was cut off. The small amounts of medicines and food that were brought in had to be left at remote spots for collection, and for payment the villagers left coins in wells such as this, to which vinegar was added to disinfect them. William Mompesson was the Rector of Eyam, and despite his own wife being one of the victims he continued to inspire the community, preaching from a rock in the open air since the church and churchyard were closed, and the dead hurriedly buried in nearby fields.*

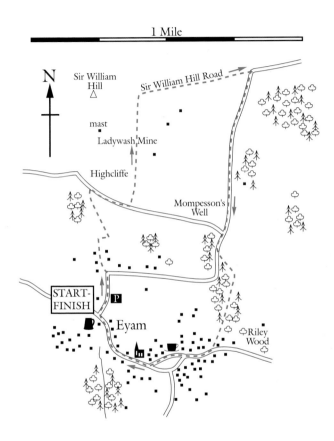

Continue down the road from the well, ignoring the turning on the right, and then a few yards later as you enter woodland take the path off to the left that descends somewhat bumpily at first down the forested hillside. At the bottom you join the end of a surfaced cul-de-sac, and carry on down this until you meet the road at the end. If you want to visit the Riley Graves, where many plague victims were buried, turn left; otherwise turn right, past the Wesleyan Reform Church, down to The Square where you will find the welcoming Eyam Tea Rooms.

Now much refreshed, resume your exploration of Eyam. The Lydgate Graves can be found down a drive to your left, or else walk across The Square and along Church Street. The Church of St Lawrence is well worth a visit, as it includes an interesting display about the plague, including Mompesson's Chair and the Plague Register, plus a range of local literature. Beyond the church are the Plague Cottages, where Eyam's first victim was claimed. It is assumed that plague-carrying fleas arrived among clothes ordered from London by George Viccars, a tailor, who was lodging here. The next to die were in the adjoining cottages.

Beyond the cottages is Eyam Hall, a 17th century manor house open to the public, beside which is a wide courtyard surrounded by various workshops and craft outlets (including leather, glass and wood specialists). Continue along the pavement of the main road and around a bend as far as Hawkhill Road, on the right, up which is Eyam Museum and car park.

# POPPIES TEA ROOM

*Quiet hamlets and wildlife-rich dales are linked together by a former railway line turned footpath*

TEA SHOP:
Poppies Tea
Room, Bank
Square,
Tideswell
Tel 01298
871083
OPEN: Daily
except Wed, all
year
MAP: OS
Outdoor Leisure 24
DISTANCE: 7
$^3/_4$ miles (13.5
km)
ALLOW: $3^1/_2$-4
hours
PARKING:
Tideswell Dale
car park, half a
mile south of
Tideswell

Although Tideswell calls itself a large village, it has most of the trappings of a small town: shops and a bank, tea rooms and pubs, plus an imposing medieval church. Known as the Cathedral of the Peak, the parish church of St John the Baptist was built entirely in the 14th century, and its churchyard contains the grave of William Newton, so-called Minstrel of the Peak.

From the Peak National Park car park south of Tideswell walk past the toilet block on the easy track down into Tideswell Dale. Ignore the left turn for the picnic site and trail, and a footbridge on the right, and instead penetrate deeper and deeper into this remote and enclosed valley. Cross the brook by the second footbridge and continue along the dale bottom as far as the road, then turn left to reach Litton Mill. Built in 1782, this stern-looking building harnessed the River Wye to power its production of textiles, but today it is

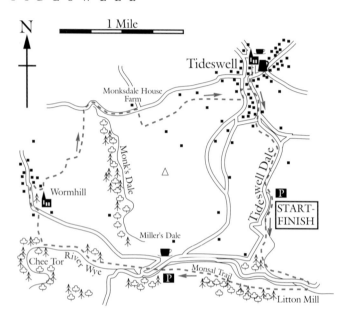

remembered for the poor treatment of its large, child workforce. Although there have been plans to renovate the disused mill building it remains a secluded and peaceful location. Cross the river by a footbridge opposite the cottages (signposted Miller's Dale) and at the top of the winding path turn right on to the Monsal Trail.

*This was Midland Railway's former London-Manchester line, now a splendid 8½ mile walking and cycling route (also see Walk 7) that is also home to banks of wildflowers, plus insects and butterflies. This is borne out by a visit to Miller's Dale Nature Reserve, a former limestone quarry just off the route that is now a valuable wildlife habitat. Approaching Miller's Dale Station the line crosses the Wye by two high, dramatic viaducts, since the station served as the interchange for*

*Buxton and had four platforms, one of them uniquely incorporating a post office. The station building and platforms have been well-preserved, and include toilets and local information, while opposite the entrance of the car park is the engaging Wriggly Tin cafe (open Tues-Fri, Feb-Nov).*

Continue along the Monsal Trail, past some interesting old lime kilns, and when you reach a small viaduct go down the stone steps on the right and at the bottom turn right again to follow the riverside track towards Chee Dale. As the valley widens there is a footbridge by a junction of tracks. Turn right, away from the river, and follow a path up the hillside until you eventually meet a road, then turn left to enter the sleepy village of Wormhill.

Just before the memorial to canal engineer James Brindley, who was born near here, turn right on the lane past St Margaret's Church. Beyond Holly House turn left at a footpath sign into a short walled passage, and at the end go over a stile and keeping the farmyard on the left cross two fields. At the far side of the second turn right and walk alongside the wall to the far end, then half left across another to join a walled track that gradually makes its way down to meet the road at the head of Monk's Dale.

With the

narrow, wooded mouth of Monk's Dale on your right, walk up the lane on the far side, with improving views down this quite wild and secluded National Nature Reserve. There is a valley bottom path through the trees all the way to Miller's Dale, but it is a rocky and time-consuming route, and is perhaps best explored on another day.

Where the road levels out, by Monksdale House Farm, turn right on to a broad, walled lane, and after 300 yards climb the wall on the left for the path to Tideswell. Indicated by the particularly eye-catching Peak & Northern Footpaths Society signpost No 217, this easy, direct route proceeds through two long fields, crosses a grassy lane, then continues across a succession of further fields before hopping over another lane and descending a field edge to the houses of Tideswell (on the way down look out for the lovely views of the mighty parish church towering above the rooftops). Turn left into the road, then right down Sunny Bank Lane, and at the bottom of this turn left again towards the shops and church.

Poppies is to be found in the centre of the village opposite the bank, and besides the usual snacks and light refreshments it serves hot meals, often into the evening. To return to the car park walk back down the main street with the shops behind you, then turn right past the Horse and Jockey pub and walk all the way down Queen Street. Go over the road at the end and continue along a track past South View Farm, then when this finishes go ahead through the gap between the fence and the wall and along the obvious path that before long drops down to the road. Turn right and walk along the pavement for 200 yards, then cross over to join a path beneath a line of mature beeches that leads back to the car park.

# D'S BREW STOP

*𝒜 n energetic walk of contrasts, from plunging limestone dales to high moorland and a converted railway path*

TEA SHOP: D's Brew Stop, Water-cum-Jolly, Cressbrook Tel 01298 872103
OPEN: Weekends, all year
MAP: OS Outdoor Leisure 24
DISTANCE: 6 ³/₄ miles (11.5 km)
ALLOW: 3 ¹/₂-4 hours
PARKING: Limited roadside parking near entrance of former Cressbrook Mill, or small car park along lane at Upperdale

Child apprentices from London workhouses once laboured at Cressbrook Mill, and despite Richard Arkwright's original building burning down, much of the Georgian architecture of its replacement remains. The River Wye was dammed to provide power for its two large water wheels, and the result is a wide, dark lake beneath spectacular limestone cliffs. The mill closed in 1965.

With the entrance of the old mill behind you turn left and walk up the lane, making sure to go right where it forks (signposted Cressbrook, Litton). The ground soon falls away to your right as the lane climbs through woodland, and when you eventually come to a hairpin carry straight on along a clear wooded path. Keep right at a fork and emerging from the trees you begin to appreciate the impressive scenery of Cressbrook Dale, none more so than the formidable cliffs opposite.

# CRESSBROOK

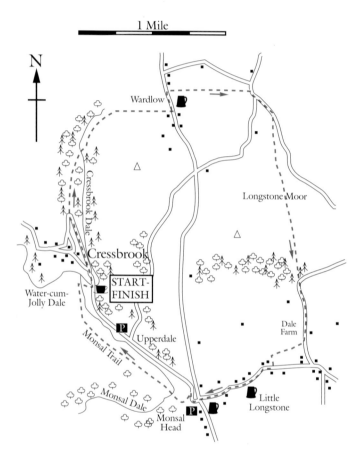

*This area is also known as Ravens Dale, after the birds that inhabited the high cliffs and crags until they became extinct from the White Peak last century.*

At the bottom of the slope go left and cross a footbridge, then make sure to keep right where the path divides and follow this rising path all the way to the top of the hillside. The views north to the head of the dale are superb, with woodland giving way to bare, plunging slopes punctured by frequent limestone scars. Ignore a grassy path that swings off left, back down the hillside, but instead go straight on and over a stile for a long, walled grassy lane surrounded by similarly narrow and elongated fields that all slope down towards the strung-out village of Wardlow. And it is here that you eventually arrive, and after carefully crossing the road turn left and walk along the pavement past the pub as far as the church. Immediately after the latter turn right into another narrow field for an indistinct but direct route via the bumps and pits of an old mining area to the lane up on the far slope. (If the immediate surface looks too muddy then simply carry on down the road for another 300 yards and take the surfaced lane right that runs parallel with the path, turning right at the junction at the far end.)

Turn right into the lane, then immediately left up another, and after 400 yards take the path off to the right. This heads through three fields towards the high, flat outline of Longstone Moor, and after the third you are out on to rough moorland. Skylarks and wheatears may keep you company, and look out too for curlews and lapwings. The narrow path climbs gradually through the heather, aiming more or less southwards across the middle of the moor.

Take a last look behind you towards Wardlow and Eyam Edge, and continue over the brow of the hill and across a wide dip that has been refilled after excavation in recent years (hence the patchy vegetation). Carry straight on,

keeping left of a ditch that becomes an embankment —
the remains of a long-disused quarry tip — then descend
to a stile and beyond for a steepening track via woodland
to a lane below. Go down this, and after approximately
600 yards turn right by a high wall for the drive to Dale
Farm. Beyond the old barn at the end cross the stile and
walk along the foot of successive fields, turning left on
the far side of a private dwelling for an overgrown lane
down to the road.

Turn right and follow the road via Little Longstone to
Monsal Head. Cross the main road and pause to savour
the breathtaking views of Monsal Dale, with the famous
railway viaduct far below. Refreshments are available
here, but Cressbrook is close at hand, and there are no
more climbs to come. And do you really want to share
your cuppa with lazy trippers who have walked no
further than the car park ten yards away?

At the tight road bend by the car park take the path
down the hillside signposted Monsal Trail and viaduct,
turning left to emerge on the former trackbed of Midland
Railway's London-Manchester line. To your left is the
sealed-up tunnel where the locos steamed through en
route for Bakewell and Buxton; so turn right for the
dramatic, 80ft high viaduct crossing of the River Wye.

*The remaining mile is mostly flat and very easy, as you chug past
the platform of the former Monsal Dale Station. The line closed in
1968, but it was later purchased by the Peak National Park who
have turned it into an 8½ mile recreational route for walkers and
cyclists (a leaflet guide is available from local information centres).
At the time of writing there is talk of exploring the feasibility of re-
opening the railway line, but it is hoped that the Monsal Trail will
remain a permanent fixture.*

When you come to another closed tunnel follow the trail to the right, along and then down the hillside to cross the river by a footbridge before the picturesque, cliff-backed lake at Water-cum-Jolly. Turn right, past the quarry yard, to reach D's Brew Stop, and beyond this is a passageway past the old mill back to the road.

*D's Brew Stop is not your traditional, quaint country tea shop. Housed in a curious old folly that was built by the mill owner to 'improve' the site, it allows you to eat your own food (outside seating only) and offers a range of local and general information for walkers in the Peak District.*

# THE COTTAGE TEA ROOM

ASHFORD IN THE WATER

*From picturesque riverside to steep woodland, with a visit to a well-preserved former lead mine*

TEA SHOP:
The Cottage Tea Room, Fennel Street, Ashford in the Water
Tel 01629 812488
OPEN:
Weekends, all year
MAP: OS Outdoor Leisure 24
DISTANCE:
5 miles (8 km)
ALLOW:
3 hours
PARKING:
Public car park, Ashford in the Water

Ashford is one of the Peak District's picture-postcard villages, but a short walk up to the surrounding hills allows even more rewarding views over the handsome Wye valley. After the walk enjoy a pot of Cottage Leaf Tea, which is actually blended on the premises by the Cottage Tea Room owners who are members of the Tea Council Guild of Tea Shops. Between 2.30-5pm there is a range of set afternoon teas, including the Cottage Tea, Derbyshire Cream Tea, Hovis Tea, and the Savoury Scone Tea. Mouth-watering certainly, but make sure you do the walk first!

Locate the tea rooms on Fennel Street, in the centre of Ashford, then go past the circular shelter and over Sheepwash Bridge. Cross the A6 with the utmost care and turn right to walk along the pavement. In 300 yards turn left on to a quiet lane signposted Sheldon, and where this soon

bends left go ahead for the wide footpath that continues beyond a gate and along the riverbank. (A broad grassy track heads up the hillside on your left, which is a shorter alternative route to the village of Sheldon that avoids the wooded ascent ahead.)

The easy and mostly level route continues for a mile along the south bank of the River Wye, at one point passing around the back of a disused mill building. After a series of pools the path veers away from the river, and about 400 yards further on at an approximate crossroads of paths turn left up into Great Shacklow Wood. The richly-wooded hillside is a delightful place, home to a range of birds, plus it is cool and shady in the summer — which is just as well since the path seems to go up and up! However, thanks to the steps constructed by the Derbyshire Dales Group of the Ramblers' Association the ascent is safe and straightforward, and when the steps end near but not quite at the top of the woods turn left for an easier path up through the trees.

Where you emerge by a gate there is a fabulous view down over the Wye valley; then go ahead through the gate and cross the field, with the wall on your left. At the

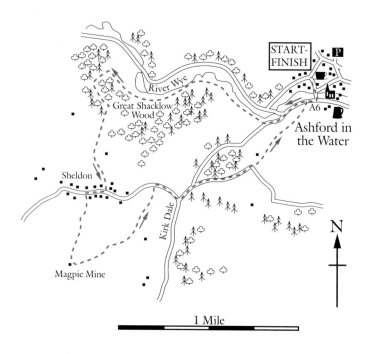

far side locate the easily-missed wall steps and on the far side follow a narrow path around the edge of some undergrowth to resume a wall-side path through the field opposite. Join a narrow, walled passage, then at the end turn left into a farm lane to reach Sheldon.

At the main street turn right and walk up through this quiet, pretty village, until just before the Hartington Memorial Hall turn left on to a signposted public footpath. This crosses three small fields, and in the last veer half-right to go through the gate in the far corner. Beyond the next field is a short walled track, and at the end of this go through the wall gap on the left for the obvious grassy track over to the distinctive chimney and buildings of Magpie Mine.

*Lead-mining has a long history in this area, reaching its peak in the 18th and 19th centuries, but it was a difficult and costly business and success was always brief. Magpie Mine, the best-preserved in the Peak District, includes the shell of an engine house and round chimney built by Cornish miners in the mid 1800s (14 of them came to live in Sheldon). Next to it, by the top of the 700ft main shaft, is the winding gear and corrugated iron shed that was erected in the 1950s and represents the most recent attempts to revive the mine. A few hundred yards away is a replica of a horse gin, a circular, wooden winding device once used to bring the lead ore up to the surface and which worked by a horse plodding round and round the 'gin circle'.*

To return to Ashford stand with the tall, circular chimney behind you and face the path back to Sheldon, then walk half-right on a faint grassy path via a small, circular stone construction and some hawthorn bushes. As you go over the wall note the direction of the yellow footpath waymark and cross the middle of the wide field before you. There is a footpath sign on the far wall for guidance, and beyond this the route continues through another field and joins a long, walled lane all the way down to the Sheldon road.

Turn right into the lane, then as this swings around to the bottom of Kirk Dale take the short path down to the left that cuts off the corner. Cross the road at the bottom for the narrow lane up the far side (indicated unsuitable for heavy goods vehicles), then shortly after the woods disappear there are stunning views down to Ashford and the Wye, and towards Monsal Head and Longstone Edge beyond. Where the lane bends right go through the gate on the left, and still soaking up the glorious panorama descend through the wide, sloping pasture via a small transmitter mast. Keep the wall on your right, and nearing the bottom of the hillside join a rough drive by a cottage which brings you out on the A6 once more. Cross with caution to re-enter Ashford — or you may wish to walk right, along the pavement beyond the bend, for a safer crossing of this busy road.

# GOOSE GREEN TEA ROOMS

BASLOW

*A* straightforward walk up and along an airy gritstone edge, with a return via fields

TEA SHOP:
Goose Green
Tea Rooms,
Nether End,
Baslow
Tel 01246
583000
OPEN: Daily,
all year
MAP: OS
Outdoor Leisure 24
DISTANCE:
4 ½ miles (7.5
km)
ALLOW: 2½ –
3 hours
PARKING:
Large public car
park near tea
rooms in Baslow

The tea rooms and car park are located off the A619 Chesterfield road next to the Devonshire Arms, at the part of Baslow known as Nether End. Despite the traffic, Baslow has a quieter side, and the waterside path past the tiny toll house into Chatsworth Park that begins around the corner from the tea rooms is particularly pleasant. But if it's views you're after nothing beats a round trip up to Baslow Edge, a high gritstone shelf that sits above the village and affords commanding views over the Derwent valley and Chatsworth.

From the car park cross the main road by the pedestrian lights and walk up Eaton Hill opposite, and at the small green at the top fork right and go up Bar Road. Continue straight uphill at a junction and soon the road becomes an unsurfaced track and leaves the houses behind. For half a mile this wide, rutted thoroughfare

*47*

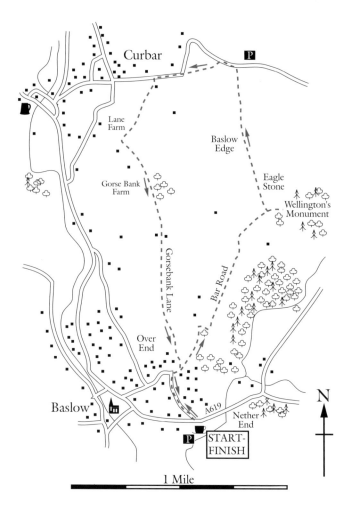

climbs its way up and eventually out on to the moors above Baslow; and at a gate a notice informs you that you are entering the Eastern Moors estate, an area of National Park-run public access land. Stay with the main track as it swings gradually right and up to the top of the moor. The views from this lofty position are superb, not least of the large Chatsworth Estate due south. In fact it may surprise you that despite the acres of open, rolling parkland either side of the river in front of the famous house there is also a significant amount of wooded hillside.

Beyond a bench the wide track bears around to the left, at which point the suitably curious can follow a path off to the right that leads the short distance to Wellington's Monument, a stone cross erected in 1866 (a similar memorial to Nelson is to be found a mile away on Birchen Edge). The main route now heads directly across the high moorland, on the way passing the curious Eagle Stone. It is said that from certain angles this large, isolated rock amid the heather resembles a bird of prey — although you have to stretch your imagination a bit, since you could quite reasonably describe it as a giant owl or perhaps a Henry Moore statue. Its vertical faces and grooves are popular with climbers who use it for practice ("bouldering" it without ropes) prior to the more serious stuff on the nearby Edges. And the local story is that once upon a time every young bachelor in Baslow had to first climb the Eagle Stone before they could marry!

Now that you are on the top it's an easy and level walk across the moor to Curbar Gap and the minor road down to the village of Curbar. However, if you have time the high but easy, edge-top path continues across the lane along Curbar Edge, affording fine views over the Derwent valley towards Eyam Moor and the heart of the Dark Peak. It's well worth a short detour; but do take care towards the very edge itself where there are some unexpected drops among the massive slabs.

Resuming the main route, walk down the lane towards Curbar, and in under 200 yards go left over a stile for a short path down through National Trust land that rejoins the same lane further down the hillside. Walk down the road past Curbar Stables and take the public footpath on

the left signposted Baslow via Gorse Bank Farm. Initially this follows the drive of Lane Farm, then at a cattle grid take the far right gate for a walled path downhill that eventually leads to a stile. Go over this and turn left for a grassy track that makes its way up to the top corner of a field, with Baslow Edge in sharp relief up to your left; then go through the gateway for the obvious route through fields ahead. At the far end pass through a wall gap in the corner by a public footpath signpost, then head sharp left across to a wall stile and steps underneath some huge oak trees.

Now routefinding is easy, as the wide track before you strides through the farmyard of Gorse Bank Farm and turns into a surfaced drive that leads back into Baslow and the junction at the foot of Bar Road. Turn right, then left, in order to return to the car park and tea room.

*Baslow is made up of five separate parts known as 'Ends' (Far, Nether, Over, Bridge and West). Nether End, where Goose Green Tea Rooms is situated, presumably developed around the northern gate of Chatsworth Park; and at Bridge End you can find a particularly elegant triple-arched stone bridge across the Derwent. The nearby Church of St Anne has on show a leather dog whip in a glass case by the door, since it was once common for churches to employ a 'dog whipper' to deter unwanted canine visitors during services. Outside, the unusual church clock commemorates Queen Victoria's Diamond Jubilee, with a face inscribed 'VICTORIA 1897' in place of numbers.*

# CARRIAGE HOUSE RESTAURANT

CHATSWORTH

*A n easy walk through the glorious Chatsworth Estate, with tea in an elegant converted stable block*

TEA SHOP:
Carriage House
Restaurant,
Chatsworth House
Tel 01246
582204/565300
OPEN: Daily, mid
March–end Oct;
Park open all year
round
MAP: OS Outdoor
Leisure 24
DISTANCE: 4 1/2
miles (7.5 km)
ALLOW: 2 1/2
hours
PARKING:
Calton Lees Car
Park, off B6012
south of
Chatsworth

One of the grandest stately houses in England, Chatsworth House is surrounded by 1,000 acres of landscaped parkland that allows you to wander amid herds of deer and ancient oak trees. The Carriage House Restaurant is one of the most stylish self-service tea rooms you will ever encounter, and if you want to visit the House or gardens you will need to allow plenty of extra time.

From the far end of the car park at Calton Lees, on the southern edge of the estate, walk along the narrow surfaced lane ('no through road') past the garden centre on the left. It swings right, then at the sharp bend left go straight on along the wide gravel track ahead. This easy, attractive lane heads purposefully up the gentle valley, with a tinkling stream accompanying you all the way.

Follow it up and through Calton Houses, after which it becomes enclosed before reaching a gate and open ground. Proceed to the right, along the foot of the slope with Calton Houses now below. Admiring the views across the Derwent valley to Beeley Moor, continue across a wide field aiming for the gate to the left of an open barn. Go through this for a short lane down to walled steps into parkland.

*What a view! Before you the park rolls away down to the River Derwent, on the far bank of which is the imposing*

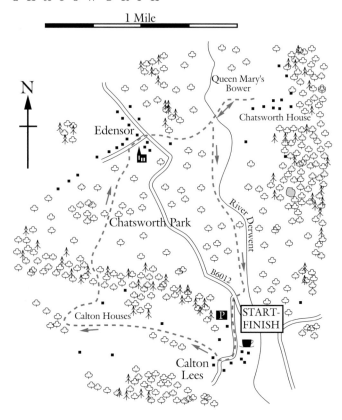

*facade of Chatsworth House and its adjoining gardens, with the tumbling water concourse known as the Cascades particularly eye-catching. Behind the House the high, tree-covered hillside of Stand Wood is topped by the distinctive Hunting Tower, while away to the north are the moors of the Dark Peak.*

When you finally tear yourself away from the spectacle

proceed down the hillside in front of you, along an obvious track that keeps to the left of two enclosed plantations (fenced to keep the deer out). After the second, much larger enclosure resist the urge to drift down to the road, towards the House, but instead veer left and make for the spire of Edensor Church. Go through the gate to the left of it (indicated by the sign 'footpath'), then down steps to the road, and turn right into the centre of the village.

*The first impression of Edensor (pronounced 'Enzer') is of a village almost too neat and ordered, isolated in the middle of the Chatsworth Estate. And this is the reason for its peculiarity, for in 1839 the 6th Duke of Devonshire decided that the old settlement of Edensor was too unsightly, so he had it repositioned and reconstructed as a model estate village! St Peter's Church was also rebuilt last century, and at the top of the churchyard is the grave of Kathleen Kennedy, sister of the United States President (he once visited the site), who married the Duke of Devonshire's brother but was killed in an air crash.*

Go out of the main gates to the village and across the road for the wide gravelled track opposite which crests a low wooded ridge and drops down to cross the road bridge in front of Chatsworth House. Then detour left to inspect Queen Mary's Bower, a curious, raised stone platform, with an elaborate staircase. It was an Elizabethan construction and is purported to be where Mary, Queen of Scots, was taken for regular exercise during her spells of captivity at Chatsworth.

*The original Chatsworth House was built in the 1550s for the renowned Bess of Hardwick, but was much altered by subsequent members of the Cavendish family who have lived here for over 400 years. In fact the only remnant of Elizabethan Chatsworth is the Hunting Tower on the wooded hilltop behind. The interior of the house is richly and extravagantly decorated, containing a staggering array of works of art from old masters to neo-classical sculpture. A look around inside will invariably take some time, as will a tour of the garden, whose 100 acres includes fountains, rose gardens, a maze, and much more. For refreshment proceed up to the signposted Carriage House Restaurant, which occupies a former stable block and serves a wide range of snacks and drinks.*

Re-cross the bridge in front of the house, then turn left to leave the road and follow the open, right-hand bank of the meandering Derwent downstream. From here you have a close-up view of the grand West Front, although in the early days of the house the main frontage was in fact the opposite, eastern side. In the garden beside the house is a lake, and if you are lucky you may see the giant waterspout erupt into the air. When you reach a tree-lined weir take the rising track along the top of the slope above the river, passing several giant and rather dilapidated oak trees. Scattered throughout the park, they represent the western edge of old Sherwood Forest, and a few of the specimens are believed to be approaching 1,000 years old.

Walk past the waterfall and rapids as far as a ruined building that until as recently as 1952 was a working corn mill, then turn right and follow the path uphill and back to the car park.

# THE COUNTRY PARLOUR

*A fairly demanding but fascinating walk from a riverside mill up to a moorland plateau rich in Neolithic remains*

TEA SHOP: The Country Parlour, Caudwell's Mill, Rowsley
Tel 01629 734374
OPEN: Daily, Mar-Dec; weekends only, Jan-Feb
MAP: OS Outdoor Leisure 24
DISTANCE: 6 miles (9.75 km)
ALLOW: 3 $\frac{1}{2}$ – 4 hours
PARKING: Caudwell's Mill (tea room and mill visitors only)

The restored, water-powered flour mill at Rowsley is one of the few of its kind still operating in the country. Built in 1874, the mill used what was then the new technique of processing the wheat using giant steel rollers, rather than the traditional grinding by millstones. Caudwell's Mill still produces its own flour (for sale), and the accompanying craft centre includes a working forge, glass-blower and wood-turner.

From the car park behind the mill and tea rooms turn right into the lane and over the bridge, then at

the bend go straight on along a private road (also signposted public footpath to Stanton Lees). Continue along this easy, gentle route for about three quarters of a mile. Just after you emerge from some woodland take the signposted footpath off to the right. Go through a gate and along the bottom of the slope with the fence on your left, then soon return to the rough lane via another gate, continuing uphill past the handsome buildings of Stanton Woodhouse Farm. Go through the gate at the end and out along a wide grassy track that winds its way around the hillside past mature sycamores and oaks. Beyond two imposing stone gateposts (minus the gate, unfortunately) follow the direction of the sign across pasture to reach a metal gate, beyond which a fenced path leads you safely along the high rim of the disused Endcliffe Quarry.

Turn right on to the surfaced lane and follow this uphill, turning left at a junction, and when you finally approach a quarry near the top of the hill take a path indicated left across a field to woodland. Once in the trees take the path to the right which heads purposefully alongside a field towards the moor, soon offering glimpses out across the Derwent valley. Without crossing the fence on your right, continue as far as the tower.

*This folly is known as Grey's Tower or the Reform Tower, since it was built to commemorate the 1832 Reform Bill passed by the Whig Prime Minister Earl Grey. Today the doorway and window are walled-up, and it must puzzle many a motorist driving along the A6 far below.*

Go behind the tower and over a stile, turning left to follow a clear path between the heather and bracken out across Stanton Moor. It's a curious place, more akin to

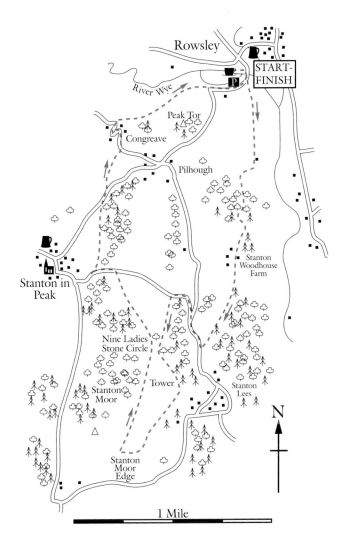

the Dark than the White Peak: a small, isolated upland gritstone plateau of odd-looking rocky outcrops and Neolithic remains. There are expansive views of the surrounding countryside, none more so than from Stanton Moor Edge, which you reach after half a mile by keeping left at a fork and following the path down to a stile by a National Trust sign. The high gritstone slabs beyond provide an excellent viewpoint across the Derwent towards Matlock, and south to Winster.

Re-cross the stile and take the sandy path opposite uphill past rhododendrons, soon merging with another from the right. At a broad intersection of tracks turn right, following the sign for Nine Ladies stone circle which hides among the trees on the far side of the moor.

*There are numerous Bronze Age tumuli and cairns scattered about Stanton Moor, but the most arresting is the circle of nine, small stone stumps set in a clearing among the silver birch, with a nearby standing stone known as the King's Stone. According to legend, the nine are local women who were turned to stone after dancing on the Sabbath, while the King Stone is the now petrified fiddler who accompanied them!*

Continue along the track beyond the stone circle, then where the trees end cross a couple of fields and turn left into a lane. This soon drops down into the quiet village of Stanton in Peak, but unless you want to visit the pub or village stores turn right immediately before the first building you come to and follow a neat, grassy private drive above the immaculate cricket green. Beyond the clubhouse the public footpath continues into woodland and steadily drops down the hillside to emerge on to the lane from Stanton to Pilhough. Turn right and at a handy roadside viewing platform pause to

CAUDWELL'S MILL ROWSLEY

admire the terrific panorama: Youlgreave and Lathkill Dale to the left, and the Wye valley directly ahead, with Bakewell in the far distance and much closer the elegant towers of Haddon Hall.

A signpost a few steps along the lane points you down a short, sharp grass slope, and then bearing right go through a fallen-down gateway and several fields to reach a narrow lane. Turn left and follow this downhill into the hamlet of Congreave, until at the third tight bend turn right and at the end of a short drive continue ahead through a field and down to a spinney in the shallow valley bottom. The path crosses a small stream, and via a gated path through the woodland emerges into a wide field above. Go diagonally half-right, aiming for the avenue of trees along a low and broken embankment. Here you join a wide grassy track all the way down the hillside towards the river, gradually swinging round towards Rowsley. At the bottom cross the stile by the gate and continue ahead to follow the road back to Caudwell's Mill.

*The mill tearooms, called the Country Parlour, are well-known not only for their delicious fresh meals and a wide range of cakes but for their imaginative construction. The floor is made of flagstones from local cottages, the tables and beams come from a Scottish mill, and the long, narrow wooden seats were once the pews of the chapel at the village of Crich Carr, south of Matlock.*

# MEADOW COTTAGE TEA GARDEN

*E*njoyable
and easy
riverside paths
along classic
limestone dales,
linked by fields

TEA SHOP:
Meadow Cottage
Tea Garden,
Youlgreave
Tel 01629
636523
OPEN: Tues-
Sun, Apr-Sept;
weekends only,
Oct-Mar
MAP: OS
Outdoor Leisure 24
DISTANCE: 6
miles (9.75 km)
ALLOW:
3 hours
PARKING: Top
of Holywell
Lane, Youlgreave,
or free car park at
western end of
village

Although the signs say 'Youlgreave' the locals prefer the more traditional 'Youlgrave', but either way this attractive, linear village is in a wonderful situation between the lovely limestone dales of the Rivers Bradford and Lathkill. No walk in this area would be complete without a waterside wander in the company of dippers and jumping trout, and it's rounded off with a visit to the Meadow Cottage Tea Gardens which surely boasts one of the best views of any Peak District cafe.

*Before you begin your walk take a moment to inspect the curious funnel-like landmark behind railings in the centre of the village. Known as the Fountain, it is in fact a large water storage tank built in 1829 when piped water was first supplied to the village. In those days it cost villagers the annual sum of sixpence to draw fresh*

*water between the hours of 6am-6pm, and even today
Youlgreave still has its own private water company that draws
water from local springs.*

Beginning in Fountain Square, face the Youth Hostel
(situated in the former Co-op building) and turn right,
then 100 yards along Main Street turn left into Holywell
Lane, and almost immediately left again after the Wesleyan
Chapel into Brookleton. Walk down to the end of this cul-
de-sac and through the wall gap for a long, sloping path
down to the River Bradford. At one spot below you the
river is dammed to allow a few hardy souls the chance of
an open air swim. Turn left at the bottom to go through
the gate and straight on across the road to resume the wide
path downstream past a well-preserved packhorse bridge.

Where the track bears right go straight ahead, through a wide kissing gate, and continue along the popular riverside track all the way to Alport.

*Before reaching Alport the track passes below a striking rock face known as Raenstor or Ravenstor Rock. Look carefully at its foot and you may just make out the date 1753 carved into the stone. It was probably the work of local miners who were commemorating the completion of a local sough (a drainage tunnel) dug to drain water from the Alport lead mines — the best known was called Hillcarr Sough which at over four miles was the longest in Derbyshire. However, the complex network of tunnels and shafts were also found to be behind the mysterious disappearance of the River Bradford in 1881, which overnight vanished into the ground near here. It was eventually discovered that the river was re-emerging several miles away at Darley Dale where it flowed into the Derwent and not the Wye.*

Cross over the road at Alport and resume the path beyond the white gate, having now left the Bradford for the Lathkill. Head through a succession of fields, and after passing below the rather austere Raper Lodge, continue along until you meet a surfaced lane. Turn right and cross the ancient Conksbury Bridge, perhaps stopping in the middle to look down at the pools below and marvel at the size of the trout, described by Charles Cotton as the reddest and best in England. The fishing, it need hardly be said, is private! The path resumes on the far bank, and simply follow the wide and easy riverside path upstream.

*The dale is now much narrower, although unlike the bare cliffs, scars and screes further upstream the steep slopes are mostly cloaked in woodland. Lathkill Dale is justly famous as one of the most unspoilt in the Peak District, and its ancient woodland is home to*

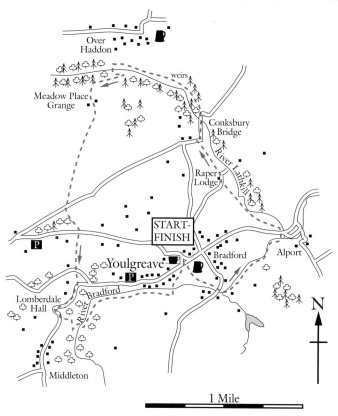

1 Mile

*a range of birdlife, including woodpeckers, warblers and owls, plus some fascinating fungi; while on the water you will see coots, moorhens, and grebes busying themselves among the rushes. In addition, the Lathkill is virtually the only Peakland river that rises and flows entirely on limestone, so that the purity of the water attracts fairly unusual specimens, such as the freshwater crayfish.*

If you have managed to tear yourself away from the wide, grassy bank that overlooks a series of delightful weirs then continue as far as Lathkill Lodge. The metalled lane on the right leads steeply up to the village of Over Haddon, where there is an English Nature information centre about Lathkill Dale, plus various refreshment points. Otherwise cross the river by the old stone footbridge and ascend the wide track through the trees. At the top you emerge into a field, where a sign points you across to the left towards the farm buildings of Meadow Place Grange. In the Middle Ages this was a busy monastic settlement, where Augustinian monks of Our Lady of Meadows (from Leicester) reared sheep and dispensed charity to passing travellers.

Go through the first of two gates between farm buildings in order to cross the wide farmyard, then leave via a couple more on the opposite side. At the foot of the open field fork half-right (the sign says Middleton & Moor Lane) and follow the straight path diagonally across this and two further fields; then go across a lane and continue through more fields and some trees. Cross a second lane and go through a wall gap opposite to descend through more fields (keep to the right of the wall all the way down) and cross the road at the bottom with care. Go over the stile and across the field below in order to turn right on to the lane to Middleton. Walk along the pavement for about 500 yards past Lomberdale Hall, and at the tight bend leave the road for a path on the left that winds its way steadily down to the River Bradford far below. Go over the bridge and turn left, and follow the riverside track down to and across the clapper bridge at the foot of Holywell Lane. The irresistible Meadow Cottage Tea Garden (outside seating only) is a few paces up the lane, and the village centre at the top.

# ELTON CAFE & GUEST HOUSE

*A close look at a curious hilltop rock formation, plus a stone circle and hermit's cave for added interest*

TEA SHOP:
Elton Cafe &
Guest House,
Moor Lane,
Elton
Tel 01629
650217
OPEN:
Weekends, all
year
MAP: OS
Outdoor Leisure 24
Distance: 4 1/2
miles (7.5 km)
ALLOW: 2 1/2
hours
PARKING: Top
of Well Street
(beside the
church), or on
Main Street,
Elton

Amid the classic limestone scenery south of Bakewell there are a number of isolated but fascinating gritstone features, typified by Robin Hood's Stride. Surrounded by Neolithic remains (like neighbouring Stanton Moor), this bizarre rock formation has puzzled and inspired visitors ever since, although any links with the ubiquitous folklore hero are rather doubtful.

Walk down Well Street, next to Elton Church, and take the driveway on the left. Where it bends right go straight ahead through a metal gate, then head half-left down the hillside aiming for the lane at the bottom — not the other path that is indicated straight down the hillside in front of you. Turn right into the lane, and after 200 yards take the footpath on the left into the trees below Anthony Hill. There are good views across the valley to the narrow opening of Gratton Dale, a little-known place that leads into the equally concealed Long Dale.

Emerging from the trees the path enters a field and turns right to make its way alongside a tumble-down wall before bearing left across fields beneath a small rocky outcrop. Do not drop down to the farm below but instead aim to the right of a small plantation of pines above it (look for the wall stiles ahead). Beyond the plantation the right of way heads north through more fields: keep to the left of the barn and look for the wall gaps; then beyond a thin line of trees head diagonally left through a field and on the far side of the gate there are wonderful views down to Youlgreave.

However, don't descend the inviting track ahead but turn right at the intersection of paths, and follow the obvious field-hopping route down to Tomlinson Wood, at which point turn left to drop downhill towards Youlgreave. Up on your right is Harthill Moor Farm, and on the distinctive hilltop beside it is Castle Ring, an Iron Age hillfort with grassy ramparts still evident. At the foot of this hill go right, through a gate, and across pasture to reach some woods. This is the route of the Limestone Way, a long-distance footpath, which leads you through pleasant mixed woodland as far as a lane where you turn right. About 400 yards up the hill go left, opposite the farm drive, and across a couple of fields to reach Robin Hood's Stride.

*This natural gritstone outcrop consists of two high towers, which it is said resemble the chimneys of an old house or hall*

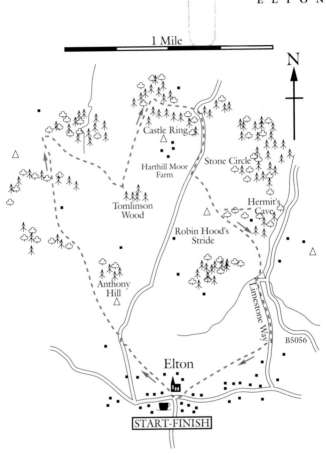

(hence its alternative name of *Mock Beggars' Hall*.) They are known as Inaccessible and Weasel by climbers, and of course the legendary outlaw is supposed to have leapt from one to the other with one massive stride (he must have been some athlete!). You are free to explore the outcrop, and its elevated position certainly affords good views of the surrounding *countryside. A couple of fields away to the north is a standing stone and small stone circle; while a signposted path to the east leads to Cratcliff Tor or Rocks, which conceals a 14th century hermit's cave incorporating a crucifix carved on its wall (when you reach the rocks at the end of the path go right and drop down quickly through the trees).*

From Robin Hood's Stride continue along the Limestone Way as it drops down towards the B5056 in the valley below. Just before you reach it go right, up a narrow and deserted lane, and after 600 yards a right of way heads

off to the right across sloping, bumpy fields in the direction of Elton. The route is not defined on the ground, but if you head towards the village centre you will meet the occasional stile and signpost and eventually come out behind the farm next to the church (with the path continuing into the churchyard behind the school). Alternatively continue all the way to the top of the lane and turn right to follow the road into Elton.

*Like nearby Youlgreave, Elton is another former leadmining village, built on the spring line between the limestone and gritstone, and although there are few buildings of any great note the Old Hall bears the date 1668 and now serves as a youth hostel. Even All Saints Church is relatively modern, since it had to be rebuilt in 1812 when the former chapel of St Margaret, constructed in the reign of Henry II, was destroyed when the spire collapsed.*

*The fact that Elton is not on the main tourist route is fortunate in some ways, as the cafe (on Moor Lane, opposite the church) has become a popular weekend haunt of cyclists and ramblers who enjoy the wide range of healthy home-made meals and snacks.*

# REGENT HOUSE

*Great views over the Derwent valley, after a long and steady climb from the bustling former spa town*

TEA SHOP:
Regent House,
35 Dale Road,
Matlock
Tel 01629
583660
OPEN: Daily,
all year
MAP: OS
Outdoor Leisure 24
DISTANCE:
4 $\frac{1}{2}$ miles
(7.5 km)
ALLOW: $2\frac{1}{2}$ –
3 hours
PARKING: Car
park by Matlock
Station
(entrance by
Derwent bridge)

Modern Matlock grew out of the Victorians' obsession with spa water, and although thermal springs do still exist locally it's the River Derwent's dramatic passage through the deep gorge downstream of the town that attracts the visitors today. From this walk you will have fabulous views of High Tor, the massive rock face that towers over the narrow river. Contrast this with the vista upstream: a wide and lush river valley, flanked by rounded moors and wooded ridges.

Turn right out of the car park, with the river behind you, and walk up Snitterton Road past the Royal Bank of Scotland. After 100 yards turn left up a drive, signposted Limestone Way/Bonsall via Masson Hill. Walk past Bridge Farm and up through a sloping field, and ignoring a turning to the left continue to the top of the field and across a small lane for a footpath on the far side. This makes its way

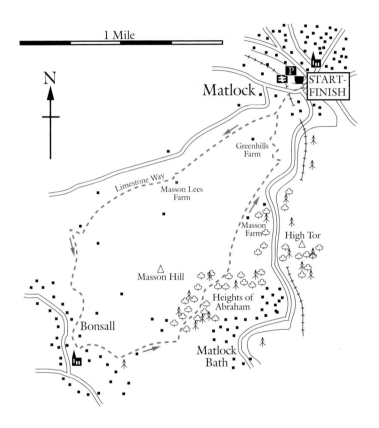

1 Mile

N

Matlock

Greenhills Farm

Limestone Way

Masson Lees Farm

Masson Farm

High Tor

Masson Hill

Heights of Abraham

Bonsall

Matlock Bath

through some trees and then follows the edge of several
fields in a steady uphill direction. In the field below
Masson Lees Farm go up the right-hand side, not the
diagonal path across the middle, and continue past the
farm and through more fields. Where a farm track crosses
go right and then left to continue up the steepening slope
— but the top of Masson Hill is almost in sight, and by

now you are rewarded with wonderful views.

*Looking back, Matlock spreads out across and up the valley side opposite. To the right is the sheer rock face of High Tor, towering above the Derwent; while behind is Riber Hill, crowned by its distinctive 'castle' — a 19th century folly that now houses a small zoo. Up the Derwent valley the views are more extensive, taking in the villages of Darley Dale, Oker and Wensley, the bulky plateau of Stanton Moor, and with the distant green ridges stretching beyond. On certain days you may hear and see the steam trains of Peak Rail chuffing up and down the valley floor from Matlock, and should you fancy a ride afterwards the station can be found beyond the car park.*

As the slope begins to level out towards the top go over a stile on the right to cross the corner of a field, then beyond a rough lane continue across the middle of more fields with the small, grassed-over dome of a reservoir behind railings on your left. After passing a barn the route enters another field and veers right to reach a stile, then after this heads left to begin a gradual descent to Bonsall. Keep to the top, left-hand edge of the rough pasture, and as the stony track begins to widen and becomes enclosed by hawthorn and other vegetation make sure to take the clear turning to the left. (If you carry on by mistake, down the sunken track under a tunnel of trees, you will finally emerge at the far end of Bonsall, and so turn left to walk along the main street into the centre.)

The easy, level route, mostly between walls, soon descends into the picturesque village nestling in the valley bottom below, eventually emerging from a surfaced track by the old market cross in the village centre.

*Ahead is the handsome King's Head, perhaps a welcome sight on a hot summer's day, but be warned that there are few other amenities in what today is a very peaceful and unspoilt place. Once, however, the village was the centre of a busy lead mining industry, and your track down from Masson Hill would have been used daily by miners.*

From the cross go up Church Street as far as St James's Church, and here turn left and walk up Ember Lane. Before long there are fine views south towards the wooded Cromford Moor, and below the transmitter mast is the gritstone outcrop of Black Rock. Where the lane swings left to Ember Farm go straight on along a dirt track, and approaching woodland turn left for the higher (ie the left) of two

75

paths that enter the trees, indicated by a Derwent Valley Walk waymark.

This long and obvious route winds its way first through an untidy patch of undergrowth and then under more attractive mature woodland, where you should ignore a fork to the left. Beyond the wood the path skirts the boundary fence of the Heights of Abraham, a touristy complex on the edge of the Derwent gorge that includes a cable car ride high above the river. On the far side follow the yellow waymarks across the entrance path as your route bounds down a grassy slope and over a wall by a white gate. The close-up views of High Tor are now superb. Continue down the hillside and around the back of Masson Farm; and after a narrow and rather slippery path besides a wall turn left on to a surfaced drive.

Upon reaching an odd-looking chapel, perched on the hillside above, fork left for a clear path that winds its way around the foot of open pasture; then with Greenhills Farm approaching up on the left go through a metal gate and stile beyond the wall on your right. The path slopes diagonally down through several fields, until half way across the last rejoin your original outward route by turning right to drop down via Bridge Farm to Matlock.

Regent House offers a range of speciality teas and coffees, plus a varied selection of sandwiches and snacks. And if you're still hungry afterwards then try the Derbyshire Larder, across the street, a well-stocked delicatessen.

# ARKWRIGHT'S MILL

C R O M F O R D

*A fairly easy walk, through beautiful hillside woodland and back alongside a canal to end at a key site of the Industrial Revolution*

TEA SHOP:
Arkwright's Mill
restaurant,
Cromford
Tel 01629
825776
OPEN: Daily,
all year
MAP: OS
Outdoor Leisure 24
Distance: 4
miles (6.5 km)
ALLOW:
2 hours
PARKING:
Arkwright's Mill
(free for
visitors) or
Cromford
Wharf

As every schoolchild will tell you, the name Arkwright is synonymous with the birth of the Industrial Revolution. The water-powered cotton mill that Sir Richard Arkwright established at Cromford in 1771 was the first of its kind, using water power from local streams to facilitate a totally new mass production process. Water was also a principal form of transport in those days, and the leafy Cromford Canal is today a lovely place to walk, with a restored steam pumping house and a railway workshop among the highlights along the way.

From Cromford Wharf car park turn right (or from the mill turn left) and walk along the pavement past St Mary's Church and over the bridge across the River Derwent. Ignore the turning on the left and continue along Lea Road to the railway bridge, then 50 yards later take the footpath on the left up steps and across a wooden stile. This climbs quite steeply through bushes and scrub until it brings you out on the side of an open, bumpy patch of hillside. Go up a little further then through a wall gap on the right for a wide path through woodland which soon emerges into pleasant open fields above the valley. In the distance the stately building on the hillside above Arkwright's Mill is Willersley Castle, once Sir Richard's private house and now a Christian conference centre.

Follow the waymarked, grassy path down past a long-fallen tree trunk, and eventually you reach a narrow lane at the bottom. Turn left and follow this past woodland until it angles sharply uphill, at which point you should proceed straight on along an obvious path below the drive of Sunnybank. Before long this pleasant track enters Bow Wood, a delightful area of luxuriant, mixed woodland that includes oak, sycamore, birch and holly. Fortunately it is in the safe hands of the Woodland Trust, and when you come to a sign explaining this continue straight on and ignore the tempting path uphill to the left.

After a while the path drops down to the road at Lea Bridge. Cross carefully and turn right in order to follow the pavement for 300 yards, then turn left on the public footpath indicated by Lea Brook House. Almost immediately go left again, by Lea Brook, for an alleyway that passes a tiny pumping station and a high wall; then turn right on to a driveway at the end. As you approach a handsome, ivy-clad building there is a small noticeboard which explains that the paved thoroughfare before you is in fact the former Nightingale Arm of the Cromford Canal, which served the mill at Lea Bridge and was constructed by the great-uncle of the famous

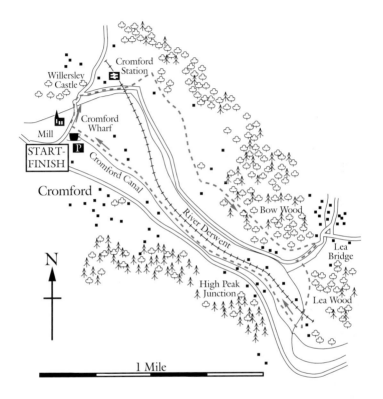

Florence (her family lived nearby).

Follow the overgrown towpath along the foot of the wooded slopes of Lea Wood — another recent purchase for the Woodland Trust after an appeal that won considerable local support — and after crossing above the railway you reach the Cromford Canal. Don't cross to the opposite bank yet, but turn right and soon the towpath brings you in sight of the distinctive tower of Leawood Pumphouse.

*The steam-driven Pumphouse was built in 1849 to maintain the water level in the canal, since water was constantly lost through boats using the flight of 14 locks that connected the Cromford Canal to the Erewash Canal at Langley Mill Basin; plus the demands on local water supplies by the Derwent mills also required the canal to replenish its stocks regularly and swiftly. The Leawood Pumphouse is 'in steam' on selected days throughout the year (usually the first weekends of the summer months), and admission is free.*

*A little further  on along the towpath you come to another relic of the industrial past at High Peak Junction. This was where the industrial plan-ners gave up the idea of continuing the canal over the high limestone plateau of the White Peak to connect with the North West, and instead they built a railway. But so difficult were some of the gradients on the Cromford and High Peak*

*Railway that wagons had to be hauled up the severest slopes using fixed steam winding engines. This was the case here, and under the road bridge at the back of the buildings you can see the beginning of Sheep Pasture Incline up to Middleton Top — there was even a catch pit at the bottom to trap runaway wagons. Today much of the former railway has been converted into the High Peak Trail, a popular walking/cycling route, and the old workshops at the canal-side location include an exhibition, snack bar and toilets.*

To return to Cromford Wharf simply follow the wide and very pleasant towpath; then beyond the preserved buildings at the end cross the road to reach the mill. The

site of Arkwright's water-powered cotton spinning mill is open all year round, and includes the tearoom, mill shop and gift shop, and although many of the original buildings are undergoing a long-term reclamation project there are regular guided tours and plenty to see.

# BARROWDALE RESTAURANT

CARSINGTON WATER

*An easy walk around a peaceful and scenic reservoir rich in wildlife*

TEA SHOP:
Barrowdale
Restaurant,
Carsington Water
Visitor Centre
Tel 01629
540363
OPEN: Daily, all
year
MAP: OS
Outdoor Leisure 24
DISTANCE: 7
1/2 miles (13 km)
ALLOW: 3-4
hours
PARKING:
Carsington Water
Visitor Centre,
off B5035
between
Wirksworth and
Ashbourne

Carsington Water occupies an open and peaceful valley near Wirksworth on the southern edge of the Peak District, and as man-made reservoirs go it is a splendid place to explore. Outdoor enthusiasts can enjoy the miles of footpaths and cycle tracks; or a range of watersports from sailing to windsurfing and canoeing. There's a Wildlife Centre and several bird hides; and the Visitor Centre includes an absorbing exhibition all about water, plus shops, cafes, and a children's playground.

The entire route around Carsington Water is excellently waymarked for walkers by yellow footprint discs, and apart from some lanes at the northern end of the reservoir all the walking is along firm and well-defined tracks. Where the route is shared by cyclists the track is wider, but of course still stay alert for these rather more faster users.

From the Visitor Centre pick up the main track that passes the car park and head north, past the Watersports Centre (not the other direction, past the Sailing Club). Very soon you will notice a looping path to the right, on the far side of which is the Wildlife Centre.

*From the Centre you can observe the birdlife off-shore using a 'live' remote-controlled camera situated on the small island ahead; plus there are details on some of the 170 different species of birds seen at Carsington Water. Winter visitors include teal, wigeon and pochard, while regulars include Canada geese, cormorants and grebes. Two of the more unusual visitors that had been spied around the time of my last visit included the little egret and black-necked grebe.*

Continue along the track as it winds its way around several bays, after which waymarks indicate that the walkers' route branches off to the right. Aspiring ornithologists may wish to make a diversion to visit the

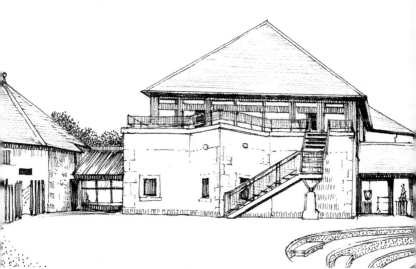

first of two bird hides, or a little further on ascend a brick viewing tower by the side of the path for grand views the length of the reservoir (the tower was constructed during World War II to observe bombing practice). Needless to say, a pair of binoculars will greatly enhance your visit!

The path heads through the middle of Sheepwash car park, and shortly after crosses the main road from Wirksworth — take appropriate care. It then continues uphill and at the corner of a narrow surfaced lane go straight on to emerge opposite the Miners Arms at the village of Carsington. Turn left and then immediately right for a short path up to the lane behind the pub. Here turn right and follow this quiet country road for three quarters of a mile past Hopton Hall, the 17th century home of Civil War activist John Gell who did much to rally Derbyshire to the Parliamentary cause. As you reach the end of the village of Hopton turn right through a gate for a short path down to and across the main road in order to resume the shoreline path.

*Carsington Water was officially opened in 1992 and is the ninth largest reservoir in England. When full it holds a staggering 7,800 million gallons — enough to keep one person in water for over 500,000 years! Most of the water is pumped from the River Derwent over six miles away, and from Carsington it is sent to treatment works before supplying households throughout the East Midlands.*

As the track heads south above the reservoir it enters a lovely area of mixed woodland, home to birds such as long-tailed tits, woodpeckers and warblers. Almost a mile of this north-eastern shore is a designated conservation area, sensitively managed by a local ranger service.

Eventually the route becomes more open and there are lovely views across the water, to the green ridge of hills northwards beyond Carsington, and opposite to the dinghies and sail boards busy on the water in front of the Visitor Centre. After Upperfield Farm, where you walk a

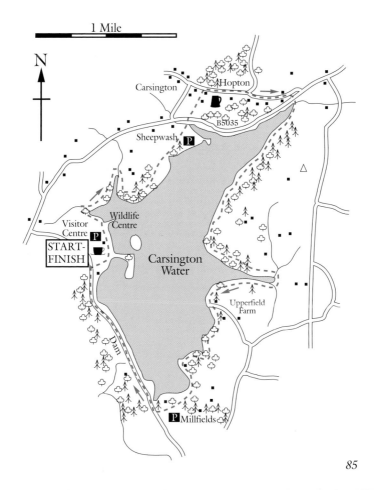

**BARROWDALE RESTAURANT**
............................................................................................................

C A R S I N G T O N    W A T E R

lane for a hundred yards or so, the walkers' route heads down towards the waterside and winds its way peacefully along the indented shoreline. As you approach the end of the reservoir you will notice a small island with a curious-looking tree in the middle of it. This is called the 'Reservoir Tree', a natural sculpture that is intended to be used by the likes of cormorants and herons, and possibly ospreys. On the shoreside path overlooking the island is a tiny shelter built out of material from farm buildings demolished to make way for the reservoir, and inside it contains a bat box.

The path eventually comes out at Millfields car park, where there are toilets and a seasonal refreshment kiosk. Beyond is a long, straight track across the length of the dam, at the far side of which you pass the Sailing Club and arrive back at the Visitor Centre. The odd-looking tower rising out of the water on your right is known as the control tower, where the volume of water flowing in and out is carefully monitored and regulated. But as you walk across the wide, flat surface, look away from the reservoir down the valley for a taste of what the area might have looked like before flooding took place.

# MANIFOLD TEA ROOM

*A scenic tour of the lower Manifold valley, from riverside parkland to breezy hilltop*

TEA SHOP:
Manifold Tea Room, Ilam Park
Tel 01335 350245
OPEN: Daily, May-Sept; weekends only, Oct-May
MAP: OS Outdoor Leisure 24, Landranger 119
Distance: 5 miles (8 km)
ALLOW: 2 ¹/₂-3 hours
PARKING: Ilam Park

The walk begins and ends in Ilam Park, managed by the National Trust whose shop, information centre and tea room can be found in the former stable block of Ilam Hall. The remains of this elegant Victorian mansion, partially demolished in the 1930s, is now a youth hostel and not open to the public; but you are free to wander the pleasant grounds, including the delectable path beside the River Manifold — along which this walk begins.

At the entrance to the car park go over the drive in order to cross the vast lawn in front of the hall. Keeping the church on your left, walk down to the old stone bridge at the far side, known as St Bertram's Bridge (after a local hermit), but instead of crossing it turn right to follow what is soon a wide and popular track along the riverbank. After you pass a second weir look out for so-called 'boil holes' on the right. This is where water from the River Manifold bubbles back up to the surface after

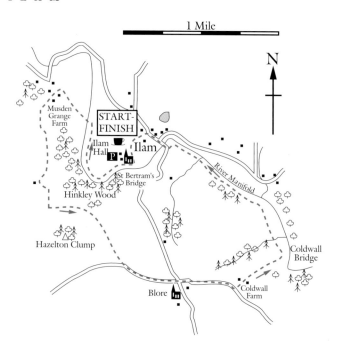

disappearing below ground some miles upstream.

A little further on is the Battle Stone, believed to be the shaft of a Saxon cross that was discovered when the village was being built last century. Across the river are the steep wooded slopes of Hinkley Wood, particularly noted for its limes, but gradually the valley opens out, and ignoring a footbridge beyond the field on the left continue to the end of the path in order to cross the river via a green metal footbridge ahead. Now follow the path half-right through several fields, with Musden Grange Farm up on your left, until you enter the final field that slopes down towards Rushley Farm. Here turn left and walk up alongside the wall to the gate, beyond which you join a rough lane to continue up past the farm.

Your route now heads up the hillside above — follow the public footpath waymarks to the right of the wall, and where this finally stops veer left. A signpost indicates the Manifold Valley circular walk to the right, but instead you should continue ahead and out along a grassy track across the open hillside. There are impressive views back over Ilam Hall to the mouth of Dovedale, guarded by the prominent green peaks of Bunster Hill and Thorpe Cloud.

The sometimes rather faint track wanders happily along the top of the sloping pasture, through a gate and all the time close to a wall on the right; and when this eventually disappears simply carry on straight ahead as the wide grassy track dips down to a gate, and then steers diagonally up the hillside opposite. With the trees of Hazelton Clump high up on your right continue along the obvious, uncomplicated route, and finally you descend to a lane. Turn left, and follow this for three quarters of a mile, through the hamlet of Blore, until at Coldwall Farm turn off left for a public footpath down the drive and through the farmyard.

The route continues beyond the farm, down a wide unsurfaced lane that emerges into a large field above the river. The grassy track before you curves gracefully down to a charming stone bridge at the bottom, and if you think this all seems a little grand for a simple farm track it is because this was once the route of the Ashbourne-Cheadle turnpike.

Don't cross the bridge but instead turn left and walk along the foot of the field (signposted Ilam). Go through a metal bar gate and ahead across another field. The path

winds its way between elder, holly and hawthorn bushes, gradually descending to the river below, until finally it surmounts a stile and returns to Ilam along the grassy riverbank. When you eventually reach the road bridge cross the river and proceed past the elaborate memorial to reach the turning for the Hall; but instead of walking up the drive go left, signposted the church, then left again on a surfaced, wallside track that brings you back to the Hall via the Church of the Holy Cross.

*The present Ilam Hall dates from the 1820s, when Jesse Watts-Russell rebuilt not just a mansion but a whole village in a distinctive mock-Gothic style. It is said that Dove Dale and its surrounding peaks reminded Watts-Russell of the Alps, which partly explains the unusual Alpine-style appearance of the village housing. In the following century the hall passed through several different hands and became badly neglected, and by the early 1930s demolition contractors had moved in. Although a large part of the hall was lost, the last minute intervention of Sir Robert MacDougall saved the remainder, which was then donated to the National Trust.*

# THE OLDE POST OFFICE TEA ROOM

ALSTONEFIELD

*A tour of the exciting limestone scenery of Dove Dale, including several sharp slopes*

TEA SHOP: The Olde Post Office Tea Room, Alstonefield Tel 01335 310201
OPEN: Daily, mid Mar-mid Nov, closed Wed & Thurs (open Thurs in July & Aug)
MAP: OS Outdoor Leisure 24
Distance: 4 1/2 miles (7.5 km)
ALLOW: 2 1/2-3 hours
PARKING: Designated car parks in Alstonefield

Although it once had a regular market and was the focus of several different packhorse routes, today Alstonefield is a quiet and charming village, and a perfect base from which to explore the dramatic limestone scenery of nearby Dove Dale. Sheep and cattle may graze tranquilly in the flat, surrounding fields, but follow the paths down into the narrow and plunging valleys and the landscape is very different.

The tea room is in the centre of Alstonefield, and with your back to the front door head right along the lane, and at the end (opposite the Community Hall) turn left and immediately left again for a narrow walled lane. At a gate go through the wall gap on the left and down the right-hand edge of the field ahead. Where the walls converge keep close to the wall on your right and follow the path steeply downhill to come out at the road at the sensibly named Dale Bottom.

Cross over for the wide, green lane that climbs back up the hillside opposite. This becomes a surfaced driveway that emerges at the hamlet of Stanshope. The imposing building on your right is Stanshope Hall, which displays some fine Georgian and Victorian features inside as well as out, and presently provides Bed and Breakfast in the most stylish of surroundings.

Turn left into the lane, and then immediately left again on to an unsurfaced track, and in under 100 yards take the signposted path (Dove Dale) across fields on the right that leads to the National Trust's Hall Dale. Now open fields give way to a narrow and dramatic limestone valley, and the path along its dry foot becomes rocky and exciting (the dale is well-known for its fossils). Hall Dale, though, turns out to be just a taster, as it issues out into Dove Dale, one of the Peak District's finest river valleys.

The grassy, tree-lined bank of the River Dove is an exquisite spot, but although your route is ultimately upstream it is best to turn right and head downstream for a little way due to two reasons. The first is that the west bank path upstream to Milldale is difficult in places and prone to flooding; and the other is that a few minutes' walk downstream is the magnificent spectacle of Ilam Rock, standing guard above the river like a giant sentinel. Cross the footbridge below it, and turn left on to the wide and easy track all the way upstream to Milldale (about a mile).

*The winding, riverside route is full of fascinating scenery, from sheer cliffs and weirdly-shaped rocks to the dramatic caverns of Dove Holes, which was once an extensive network of caves. All the time the Dove flows peacefully below, often tree-lined and*

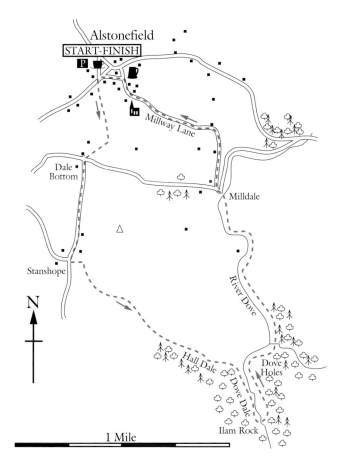

*populated by various water fowl and other wildlife.*

Approaching Milldale the track eventually crosses an old stone packhorse bridge, referred to as Viator's Bridge in *The Compleat Angler* by Isaac Walton and Charles Cotton, since the character called Viator fears it is too narrow to cross and is only convinced to proceed after much debate. On the other side is a National Trust information barn, and should you feel like pausing there is ample opportunity for an ice cream by the riverside. The final leg of the route from Milldale back to Alstonefield is up the surfaced Millway Lane from the centre of the village — turn right past Polly's Cottage and continue up past the 'phone box. Behind the latter there is a signposted footpath which cuts out most of the tarmac, but since it involves one particularly sharp ascent it is probably easier to stick to the narrow and for the most part deserted lane.

Just when you begin to wonder whether the hill will ever end it levels out and passes St Peter's Church. Now back in Alstonefield, turn left at the end to return to the attractive green in the centre of the village, with the tea rooms located just beyond the 16th century George and Dragon Inn.

# BERESFORD TEAROOM

HARTINGTON

*A generally easy walk incorporating riverside meadows, walled lanes and exquisite limestone dales*

TEA SHOP:
Beresford
Tearoom,
Market Place,
Hartington
Tel 01298
84418
OPEN: Daily,
Easter-end Oct;
Fri-Sun only,
end Oct-Easter
MAP: OS
Outdoor Leisure 24
DISTANCE:
5 ¾ miles (9.5
km)
ALLOW:
3 hours
PARKING:
Hartington
main square or
car park nearby

The River Dove is perhaps best known for its stepping stones and towering rock sentinels further downstream, but its upper reaches are also varied and fascinating, and generally a little less congested. The wide main square of Hartington, first granted a market charter by King John as far back as 1203, can also be rather busy at peak times, and might repay a midweek or out of season visit.

Leave the centre of Hartington on the lane to the Youth Hostel, by the grey-painted 'phone box, and follow this uphill before taking a turning on the right ('no through road'). Known as Reynards Lane, this narrow, walled thoroughfare runs across high pasture for three quarters of a mile until suddenly it veers right. Here go straight on, along the right of two unsurfaced lanes (signposted Biggin Dale), and beyond a handsome old barn go through a gate and continue down to the dale bottom before swinging around to the right.

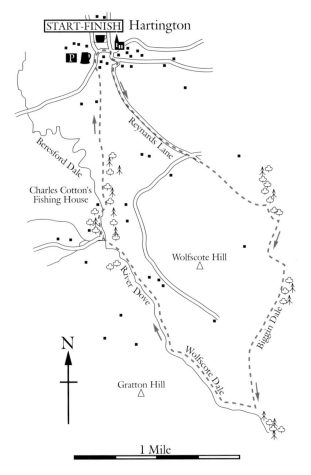

Now the scenery is very different. Biggin Dale is a narrow and dry limestone dale, incorporating a few trees but mainly clothed with scrub that includes the yellow-flowering gorse. The path veers across the grassy valley floor, and on the far side of a gate go right at a junction

of tracks signposted public bridleway to Biggin Dale
(behind the wall next to the dew pond). Although
sometimes rocky underfoot the route sticks to the dale
bottom all the way, and you can take your time and
admire the screes and caves that pit the steep sides of the
dale. Eventually, at the end, you are confronted with the
towering face of Peaseland Rocks, at the foot of which
the River Dove gurgles merrily along, making a pleasant
and noisy contrast to the dry dale behind you.  Now turn
right and follow the broad and flat track upstream along
Wolfscote Dale.

As with Biggin Dale before, there is usually a profusion
of wild flowers on the grassy slopes during spring and
summer, which of course means plenty of colourful
butterflies and insects. Meanwhile, the rocks above have
been fashioned into weird shapes, and there are
numerous natural caves and arches.

When you come to a wall go through the gap and
straight on through a meadow, ignoring the temptation
of a footbridge to the left. Continue through a wood on
the far side, where you can at last cross the Dove by a
narrow footbridge; then turn right on the far bank and
follow the clear path through the woods of Beresford
Dale and past a succession of weirs.

*The River Dove is particularly associated with Izaak Walton
and Charles Cotton, famous as authors of* The Compleat
Angler. *Although ostensibly a comprehensive study in how to
catch and cook fish, Walton subtitled it* The Contemplative
Man's Recreation *and it provides a charming portrait of
17th century rural England; indeed its popularity has
endured to this day. Cotton was born in Beresford Hall,*

*overlooking the river, and although this is no more, the fishing lodge or temple that the two friends shared while discussing the merits of various bait, rods and of course the one that got away, is still there among the trees as you leave Beresford Dale (unfortunately there is no public access to it).*

After re-crossing the tree-covered but dwindling river by another footbridge you emerge into open pasture and follow the obvious path straight on, making for the foot of a small hill ahead. This popular path is indicated by occasional, low yellow posts, which lead you up and down across several more fields and on to a clear track that descends to the road at Hartington. Turn right, past Rooke's Pottery, to regain the village centre and refreshment. Beresford Tearoom is one of several on offer, and, if you want a souvenir of this popular little market town why not consider buying a piece of the locally-produced and very tasty Hartington Cheese. The Cheese Shop, off the main square, sells a mouth-watering selection that includes Dovedale White Stilton, Dovedale Blue and Cheshire.

# THE OLD SMITHY

*A tour of upper Lathkill Dale, a quiet and peaceful haven rich in wild flowers*

TEA SHOP:
The Old Smithy,
Monyash
Tel 01629
814510
OPEN: Daily
except Monday,
all year
MAP: OS
Outdoor Leisure
24
DISTANCE: 4
miles (7.5 km)
ALLOW:
2 hours
PARKING: Car
park off Chapel
Street, Monyash

The former lead-mining village of Monyash is the perfect base from which to explore the beautiful limestone slopes of Lathkill Dale. On the way back you pass through a former monastic grange; and the walk is rounded off by a highly agreeable cafe that serves a full range of cooked food, provides daily newspapers for browsing — and outside sports the most congenial of signs: 'Muddy boots welcome!'

From the car park turn left and walk past the Methodist Chapel out towards the edge of the village. Go right at the road junction (signposted Sheldon), then in 50 yards turn off right by a farm gate for an easy footpath down the open and gentle Bagshaw Dale. At the far end cross the road and continue along a more popular path into Lathkill Dale. The dale remains low and wide, and depending on the time of year hundreds of buttercups and early purple orchids may line your route. But as you proceed through successive gates, the dale narrows and soon it becomes extremely rocky underfoot.

*The main reason for this is that you are walking over the debris from the disused Ricklow Quarry, which was once mined for ornamental limestone. When polished it becomes a distinctive grey, and this 'figured' marble, sometimes known as grey or Derbyshire marble, was popular in Victorian times when it was incorporated into the floors and stairs of large houses (including nearby Chatsworth House).*

Continue along the dale bottom track beneath ever more impressive limestone crags and cliffs. This is a classic limestone valley, with thin soils and much bare rock. Plus, of course, very little evidence of any surface water as it mostly drains away through the permeable rock. However, as the dale widens a little and swings right look out for Lathkill Head Cave off the path on your right which in winter months, at least, is often where the River Lathkill makes its first appearance. In the summer months it's usually dry and explored by pot-holers!

*Lathkill Dale is part of the Derbyshire Dales National Nature Reserve, and its unspoilt grassy slopes support a wealth of limestone-loving flowers and plants. The dale is particularly noteworthy for the rare Jacob's ladder, with its clusters of large blue flowers and ladder-like leaves. It hardly needs saying, but please don't be tempted to pick any wild flowers — take only photographs and happy memories away with you.*

Turn right and cross Sheepwash Bridge, where as the name suggests sheep were regularly washed until as recently as the 1940s. You are now leaving Lathkill Dale

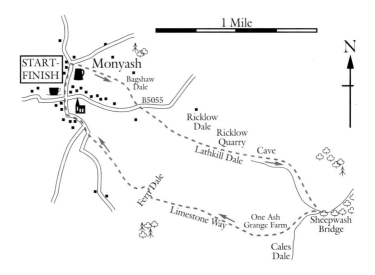

for Cales Dale, a small and much more wooded side valley. Follow the clear track up the slope, and ignoring a path down to the left continue to ascend until you emerge into a field (the curious hole in the rock to your left is probably a ventilation shaft from an old mine). Go ahead and follow the path through the large farmstead of One Ash Grange.

*Like Calling Low, another nearby farm, One Ash Grange was formerly a monastic settlement founded by Cistercian monks from Roche Abbey in Yorkshire in 1147. A grange was basically an outlying farm owned and run by a particular order of monks, and since some monastic estates could be quite vast it was not unusual for an individual abbey to manage many different granges (Furness Abbey in Cumbria held as many as 18). At One Ash Grange sheep farming was a major part of the income, although as you walk past the interesting collection of buildings you will notice a splendidly-preserved series of pig sties, and what at first appears like a cave carved out of the rock which was presumably used as a cold store or ice house.*

Proceed up the main drive past newer barns, and at the far end go through the gate into the field on the right. Ignoring the track straight ahead turn left and with the wall at first on your left walk uphill through the fields. Your route, incidentally, is part of the Limestone Way, a long-distance footpath that extends from Castleton to Matlock, with spurs to Ashbourne and Rocester. It now heads directly for Monyash through a succession of fields, finally dipping down to the shallow Fern Dale where it joins a walled farm lane. Walk along this all the way into

Monyash, going straight on when you meet the road at the end. As you approach the village green you pass Fere Mere, a clay-lined pond that once provided drinking water for livestock.

*Monyash (probably meaning 'many ash trees') was once an important lead-mining centre, although there is little evidence of it today. In the wooded, middle section of Lathkill Dale there was much mining activity in the 18th and 19th centuries, with numerous shafts sunk, and water wheels and pumping engines built, to try and drain the mines in the search for lead. In the Middle Ages Monyash had its own Barmote Court, which administered local mining affairs, and the village was granted a market charter as early as 1340.*

# LONGNOR CRAFT CENTRE & COFFEE SHOP

L O N G N O R

*O pen and mostly easy walk through two valleys, via the site of a prehistoric defence*

TEA SHOP: Longnor Craft Centre & Coffee Shop, Market Hall, Longnor Tel 01298 83587
OPEN: Daily, all year, except Jan and Feb
MAP: OS Outdoor Leisure 24
DISTANCE: 6 miles (9.75 km)
ALLOW: 3 hours
PARKING: Centre of Longnor

Longnor is a large, attractive village sitting on the edge of a sharp ridge that separates the Dove and Manifold valleys. Although the cobbled main square is flanked by several pubs the dominant building is the former Market Hall, and above its entrance is a list of the dues once payable by stallholders and buyers. Today the building houses the excellent Craft Centre & Coffee Shop, which in addition to a range of tasty fare offers visitors an interesting showcase of furniture, artwork and other crafts.

Leave the main square in Longnor

along the road past the fish and chip shop, and turn left up the alleyway after the Cheshire Cheese Hotel car park entrance. At the top turn right then left and go up the road with the new-looking bungalows on your right. At the top turn left into a lane, and very shortly fork right (signposted bridleway) that plunges down the steep hillside. Before you is the stunningly beautiful valley of the River Dove, a green and narrow corridor that winds its way into the heart of the White Peak.

Where the lane bends right at the foot of the slope go around the left hand side of the barn and head out over the open field towards the far side of the valley. Cross the infant Dove by Beggar's Bridge, and then at the far end of a green lane don't join the farm drive but instead cross into the field on your right and follow the white-marked route through a couple of fields before joining a track that passes a farm to reach a road. Turn right into the hamlet of Crowdecote, then after going down the main road past the pub for a few yards turn left by Toll Bar Cottage on to a short no-through road. Follow the track below Bridge End Farm and ignoring the turning down to the bridge carry straight on through a gate, signposted public footpath to Pilsbury.

The route is now direct and open, across a series of wide fields with the meandering, tree-lined Dove below to your right. The bare valley side above is quite wild, and as you approach the curious earthworks known as Pilsbury Castle Hills pause and take a look behind at the distinctive peak of Chrome Hill in the far distance. The angular hills and ridges that dominate the head of the Dove valley are formed from reef limestone, a tough and highly resistant rock rich in fossils that originated as coral-type deposits in the Carboniferous sea around 330 million years ago.

*The public footpath heads to the left (above) the lumpy, hillside earthworks, but close proximity does not necessarily reveal the secrets of this enigmatic site. Although there was once a motte and bailey defensive work here for certain, the exact origin is something of a mystery, although it is generally supposed that it was the location for some sort of Iron Age hillfort. One of the problems is that the ground has never been properly excavated, and there are no plans to do so today.*

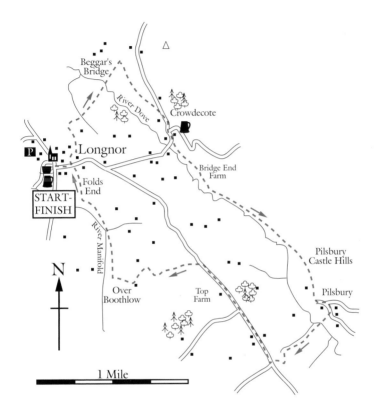

*Infuriating for archaeologists maybe, but at least your imagination can still wander happily.*

Go over the stone stile behind the Castle Hills and turn right to follow the path by the wall into the hamlet of Pilsbury. Join the lane downhill, and beyond a gate turn right for a bumpy track down to a footbridge across the river. Since the Dove is the county boundary, leave Derbyshire to return to Staffordshire and follow the climbing, rutted track all the way to the top of the hill. This is the only major ascent of the walk so take your time! At the top turn right and walk along the high and breezy lane for three quarters of a mile. To your left is the valley of the River Manifold, its gentle open shape reflecting its clay-based shale composition; whilst the River Dove has had to carve out a narrow and often severe course through the hard and resistant limestone.

About 400 yards beyond the white-washed Top Farm turn off the road to the left for a gated farm lane. At its end go ahead into the right-hand field, and progress downhill with the wall close on your left. Beyond the decrepit stone cattle trough swing around to the right and drop down to go through a gate. A signpost then points you sharply leftwards, down a grassy track, and through the courtyard of Over Boothlow farm. Go round to the right, so that you emerge on the open drive down through a field to the river. Half way across turn right at an old, isolated pair of stiles and follow a long and direct path across a succession of fields ever closer to the Manifold (look for the wall gaps straight ahead). The route finally swings right, up through more fields and via the metal gated farmyard of Folds End Farm, before following the farm drive back up to the centre of Longnor — turn left at the top to reach the coffee shop.

# ROACHES TEA ROOMS

*A long the panoramic top of a famous rocky ridge and back via moorland*

TEA SHOP: Roaches Tea Rooms, Paddock Farm, Upper Hulme, near Leek
Tel 01538 300345
OPEN: Daily, all year
MAP: OS Outdoor Leisure 24
DISTANCE: 5 $^1$/$_2$ miles (9 km)
ALLOW: 3 hours
PARKING: Limited spaces in lane below The Roaches; or Park and Ride service from Tittesworth Reservoir (follow signs)

On weekends and Bank Holidays (April-Oct) the Peak National Park runs a useful Park and Ride service to the foot of The Roaches from Tittesworth Reservoir Car Park near Meerbrook, since parking is limited on the narrow lane that runs from Upper Hulme via the tea rooms to the rocks. For years climbers and walkers have been drawn to this fascinating outcrop on the Peak District's south western edge, but despite appearances you don't have to haul yourself up by ropes to savour the views!

From the bus stop amid the parking bays on the lane below The Roaches, go through the gate and walk up the wide path towards the end of the rocks. Take the path off left to reach the Don Whillans Memorial Hut, nestling at the foot of the crags, and with a massive boulder before it with ready-cut climbers' holds. The path continues to the left of the building and up through the firs, and you should make for the narrow staircase ahead/left that ascends to the lower

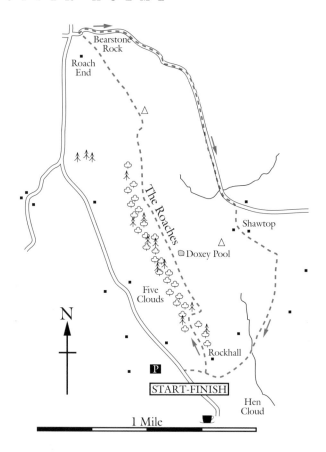

tier of rocks. Here turn left and follow the path along the foot of a higher and even more impressive series of gritstone faces, almost certainly being assailed by any number of agile and single-minded young men and women. The Roaches is one of the most popular locations for climbing in the Peak District, due in particular to the variety of climbs it offers.

An easier and rather less risky way to the top is to follow the path along the foot of the cliffs, above the trees, until it reaches a gap and cuts back up to the ridge top without difficulty. After this it becomes a wide and easy route for the entire 1½ miles of the edge until it drops gradually down to meet a road at the far end.

*The views from this lofty position are superb and immensely varied: Tittesworth Reservoir and Leek to the south, the Cheshire Plain and Mersey Estuary to the west, while eastwards stretch the bare and rolling moors of the Peak National Park south to the Staffordshire Moorlands. The rounded lines of the last are dramatically broken by the serrated edge of Ramshaw Rocks in the middle distance. When you reach Doxey Pool, a tiny circle of water by the side of the path that is as murky as its legend concerning a mermaid, look back along the path for a classic profile of The Roaches themselves, appearing like a row of heavy artillery waiting to fire a mighty salvo — the giant outlier at the far end is known as Hen Cloud. The name 'Roaches', incidentally, comes from the French word 'rocher', meaning rock, which was originally bestowed by French monks who had an abbey nearby.*

At the conclusion of the path turn right and walk along the single-track, unfenced lane through open moorland and rough pasture for a little over a mile. Just beyond a cattle grid turn right through a gate and go up a farm drive, signposted public footpath. At the second gate follow the path to the left that keeps to the outside of the boundary fence below Shawtop, and beyond the farm continue across what is sometimes rather boggy ground alongside a fence. This swings right, then a little further on go over a stile by a gate on the right and follow a farm

track until it bears left down to buildings. Here go straight
on, over a stile, for a clear path through the heather that
soon reveals a splendid view of Tittesworth Reservoir
framed between Hen Cloud and the main Roaches ridge.

When you reach the gap between the hills, by a stile in
the wall on your left, there is a choice of routes. The
main route continues ahead and down the hillside back to
the road below The Roaches — you can take a minor
short cut by following the wall on the left down to the
stile in the corner if you like. Then turn left and walk the
lane to reach the tea rooms (an easy half mile!).

Alternatively, the more energetic may wish for a brief but
panoramic diversion. Go left over the stile, across a small
field to surmount another, and then up the path on to
Hen Cloud. The views from the 1,345ft top are
spectacular but the drops are sharp, so be careful! The
easiest and safest way to descend is to retrace your
steps to the main route, and drop down to the lane.

# BROOKSIDE
# TEA ROOMS

*A short but energetic ascent of the outlying eastern peak of Shutlingsloe*

TEA SHOP: Brookside Tea Rooms, Wildboarclough Tel 01260 227632
OPEN: Wed, Sat & Sun, Easter-Oct; Sat & Sun only, Nov-Easter
MAP: OS Outdoor Leisure 24
DISTANCE: 4 1/2 miles (7.5 km)
ALLOW: 2 1/2-3 hours
PARKING: Clough House car park, on lane north of Wildboarclough

Shutlingsloe is one of those eye-catching hills, a mini Matterhorn — in shape at least. Luckily it's a good few thousand feet lower and no mountaineering skills are necessary to reach its breezy summit, from where the views over the Cheshire Plain and the moorlands of Staffordshire and the eastern Peak District are superb.

From Clough House car park turn left down the lane, and then take the public footpath to the right signposted 'Langley via Shutlingsloe'. The bulky but symmetrical outline of the distinctive hill rises above, but for now you can enjoy a quite level and easy track that winds its way above woodland and continues beyond Bank Top cottage, where it joins its short drive as far as the gate at the far end. Here turn sharply right to walk up the open drive towards Shutlingsloe Farm, and in under 300 yards turn off left for the obvious path in the direction of the summit of Shutlingsloe above.

Soon the walled pasture is left behind and the path plods steadily uphill (ignore the turning to the right). Towards the top the ground steepens and becomes eroded in places. Apart from wet weather conditions it's not particularly perilous, but as any experienced walker will tell you take the slopes slowly and steadily and you'll arrive at the top safely and in better shape than those that charge for the summit.

*At 1,659 feet Shutlingsloe is lower than both Mam Tor and Kinder Scout, but the views are no less impressive, and given its more south-westerly location there are different and interesting vistas. Near the Ordnance Survey trig point on the wide, flat summit there is a view indicator set in the rock that helps pinpoint some of the major features: The Roaches, Mow Cop and Tittesworth Reservoir to the south; westwards over the Cheshire Plain to the mountains of North Wales and the Mersey Estuary, while much closer is Croker Hill with its distinctive transmitter mast. Swinging northwards the panorama includes Macclesfield Forest and Tegg's Nose Country Park, while further round are Shining Tor and Axe Edge and the dark moorland ridges of the western Peak. Immediately below you is the tiny settlement of Wildboarclough, huddled secretively in the woods, and a little above it is the stately pile of Crag Hall.*

From the summit you have two options. The most obvious is to simply retrace your steps down the hillside as far as the farm drive at the foot of the hill, which would knock half a mile or so off the overall distance. However, a more interesting descent is to leave the

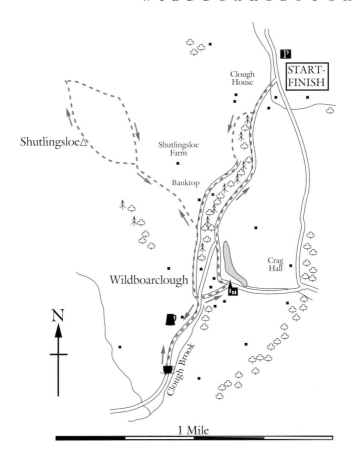

summit northwards, down rough stone steps that lead to
a line of flagstones alongside a wall. Don't cross the stile
at the far end but instead turn sharply right, signposted
Wildboarclough, and walk across a small patch of what is
occasionally rather boggy moorland, past a tiny wooden

enclosure. Keeping Shutlingsloe summit on your right, walk down a short gully, with its smooth dark sides of shale. At the bottom go half-right and cross a wall via a high stile, and continue until you rejoin the main summit track, where you should turn left and drop down to the drive from Shutlingsloe Farm.

Walk down the farm drive and instead of turning left to return directly to the car park continue straight on and down to the lane at the foot of the valley. Turn right and walk past the pub to reach Brookside Tea Rooms, a lovely old cottage nestling in the scenic and peaceful hillside, where you can reward yourself after the exertions of the last hour or so.

Afterwards walk back up the lane as far as the road bridge, rebuilt in 1989 after it was washed away when the seemingly innocuous Clough Brook became swollen by heavy rain.

*Water power was also the deciding factor behind the development of textile production in Wildboarclough in the early 19th century. Clough Brook was harnessed to power a 30-ft water wheel, and a small reservoir was also built (it is still there behind the church). The calico-printing factory that evolved later switched to producing carpets, but as the Industrial Revolution marched remorselessly on, steam power soon rendered remote water mills such as the one here at Crag Mill obsolete, and in 1860 operations ceased.*

Cross the bridge and walk up the road, past a grand, three-storey building on the left that was once part of the mill complex and later housed the village post office. Turn left in front of the church and follow the track around the churchyard, then past the old school house and some former mill cottages before rejoining the metalled lane alongside Clough Brook. Follow this back up to the car park.

# NATIONAL TRUST
# COFFEE SHOP

L Y M E   P A R K

*An easy ramble through the handsome, rolling parkland of Lyme Country Park*

TEA SHOP:
National Trust
Coffee Shop,
Lyme Park
Tel 01663
766492
OPEN: Daily,
Apr-Oct;
weekends, Nov-
Mar
MAP: OS
Outdoor Leisure 1
Distance: 4½
miles (7.5 km)
ALLOW:
2 hours
PARKING:
Station
approach,
Disley; or
Lyme Park

The walk is described as beginning and ending at Disley, but you can also start at the car park near the tea rooms in Lyme Park itself (£3.30 per car, National Trust members free), entrance off the A6. This may be more suitable if you want to visit the House afterwards (open Apr-Oct, Fri-Tues). The Park is open daily all year round and entry is free to those on foot.

Behind the small and rather unlovely Disley Station building are some fenced steps, next to a Keep Disley Tidy sign. Go up these into woodland, and at the top proceed through a gate and up the lane ahead, then where it bends right turn left (by the pillar box in the wall), past the whitewashed old vicarage. Almost immediately veer right on to a pleasant lane that soon emerges between open fields. Called Green Lane, it passes a lovely row of cottages on the left, while on the distant skyline beyond is the dark outline of Kinder Scout. To your right Horse Coppice and Bollinhurst Reservoirs come into view, with Lyme Country Park beyond. On the hilltop above is a most extraordinary building called The Cage — but more about that later.

After a while the lane narrows, then beyond a gate it becomes a rougher path and shortly afterwards meets a junction of tracks by another gate. Go through the gate and turn right down the sunken lane, not across the open ground before the gate, as the signpost to North Lodge indicates. This pleasant if bumpy lane crosses the diminutive Bollinhurst Bridge before climbing to East Lodge and entering Lyme Park. Continue along the easy drive ahead which will eventually bring you out at the front of the majestic House.

As you entered via East Lodge you may have noticed the high boundary walls, since Lyme Park has its own herds of red and fallow deer. The best place to see them is on the rough hillside above East Lodge, and the expanse of Park Moor beyond. Around September if you're lucky you can watch the stags rutting; and notices also explain that periodic deer culling has to take place (only when the park is closed). If you want to explore more of Lyme Park leaflets and maps are available from the information centre near the House.

Outside the front entrance of the House walk down the steps and cross the road to reach the Mill Pond and Coffee Shop beyond. This clean and spacious self-service cafe will provide all the refreshment you need — and don't worry, it serves tea as well as coffee! And if you choose to tour the House you will also have the option of visiting the Hall Tea Room (open Fri-Tues, Apr-Oct).

*Set in 1,400 acres of parkland and moorland, Lyme Park was originally part of the Royal Hunting Forest of Macclesfield, but after a grant from Richard II it became the ancestral home of the Legh family who developed the medieval house into the grand Palladian mansion that we see today. The interior is as lavish as you would expect, with fine tapestries and carvings; and there is also a colourful garden that includes an Edwardian rose garden and Orangery. Such is the attractiveness of the property and its setting that Lyme Park featured as Mr Darcy's House in the recent BBC adaptation of Jane Austen's* Pride and Prejudice.

To return to Disley walk up the broad, grassy ridge opposite the entrance to the House, and along to The Cage.

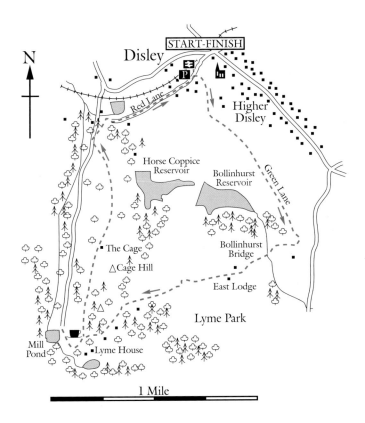

This prominent, but very odd three-floored building was built between 1733-35 originally as a banqueting house. Over the next couple of centuries it was variously used as an observation tower for watching the stag hunt, lodgings for the park's gamekeepers, and even a temporary prison for poachers. Eventually it became derelict and was abandoned but in the *last couple of years the National Trust has restored the building to its original state, and from the summer of 1999 it should be open to the public.*

Continue along the open ridge, very popular with kite-fliers, from where there are terrific views over Greater Manchester to the encircling Southern Pennines. Follow the wide track as it gradually begins to descend, then nearing the main drive at the bottom, fork half-right for a grassy path down to the ticket booth near the park's main entrance. Here go right, and up to and through the black gates by Red Lane Lodge; then simply walk this quiet thoroughfare (or at least once you've passed the kennels!) for half a mile until it bends sharply left. For those who have begun the walk in Lyme Park go straight on, turning right beyond the whitewashed old vicarage; or to return to Disley go left, then at the next bend go through the gate on the left for the steps back down to the station.

# TWENTY TREES CAFE

*A stimulating ramble up to the foot of Kinder Scout, and back across the moors*

TEA SHOP:
Twenty Trees Cafe, 3 Church Street, Hayfield
Tel 01663 745464
OPEN: Wed-Sun, all year
MAP: OS Outdoor Leisure 1
DISTANCE: 5 1/2 miles (9 km)
ALLOW: 3 hours
PARKING: Large public car park off Hayfield by-pass

Hayfield is a popular starting point for walks on to Kinder Scout, a vast upland tract of peat and bog that at over 2,000ft is the highest part of the Peak National Park. In recent years access agreements have allowed walkers the freedom to roam across much of this area, but it was not always so. Hayfield was the starting point for the much-celebrated mass trespasses of the 1930s, when ordinary men and women protested against the wholescale closures of the moors for grouse shooting. Today walking is one of the most popular recreational activities, and should you fancy a short stroll afterwards you could always leave the car park in the other direction on the 2 1/2-mile Sett Valley Trail (a converted railway line) to New Mills.

Go through the underpass that links the car park to the village centre, and turn right to walk up the main street. Towards the top turn left, opposite Fishers Bridge, and immediately left again into Valley Road. Follow this quiet road for

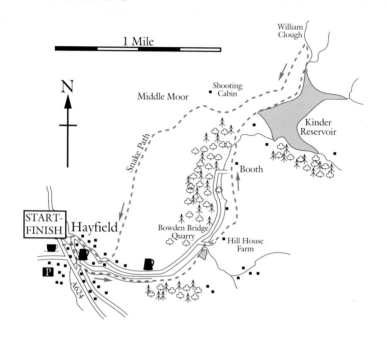

almost half a mile until it begins to peter out, and at a fork go half-left for a track that continues above the river. Stick on this purposeful route close to the water and ignore turnings off until you come to a left fork indicated 'Kinder via reservoir'. This skirts the edge of the Camping & Caravanning Club's attractive Hayfield site, and at the end of the drive by public toilets turn left over the bridge to visit the quarry car park opposite.

*Attached to the wall of the quarry is a small plaque commemorating the mass trespass of 24th April 1932, when over 400 men and women from industrial Manchester and Sheffield embarked on an organised trespass of the private*

*grouse moors of Kinder Scout. One group left Hayfield,
rallying at this quarry beforehand, and another set off from
Edale, and despite a few scuffles with gamekeepers the trespass
was successful. However, when the group returned to Hayfield
six people were arrested and subsequently jailed — by a jury
composed mainly of landowners. It was a high price to pay, but
the access movement soon snowballed and slowly the forbidden
moors of the Dark Peak were opened up.*

Return across the bridge and follow the lane as it bends left
then right, and at the junction at the far end turn left. Go up
the drive and on through the charming buildings of Hill
House Farm, and ahead through a gate and along an open
and easy farm lane all the way to Booth Farm. Continue
through more gates to cross the farmyard and follow the lane
down to the left, then very soon turn right for a pleasant
riverside path through woods. Before long this ends at a
footbridge, on the far side of which is a short path through
rhododendrons that comes out near the huge grassy dam of
Kinder Reservoir. Follow the stone-pitched bridleway behind
the pumping building and along the shore of the reservoir.

*With the water in the foreground, the views across to Kinder Scout
are impressive. The apparent dent in the long, dark ridge is
known as Kinder Downfall, where during bad weather the water
seeping off the vast peaty morass is whipped into the air as the
wind funnels through the tight gap.*

At this point there is the option of shortening the route by
about a mile by taking the track uphill to your left; otherwise
continue along the water's edge route until it veers away
toward William Clough. Go through a gate and as you
approach a wooden footbridge and a National Trust sign
turn back on yourself for a narrow path diagonally uphill.

This joins a firmer track and levels out, then traverses the hillside high above the reservoir, with even better views. Stick to the lower track where it forks, and follow it over the brow of the hill to reveal a huge area of heather moorland, a most obtrusive white shooting cabin, and maybe the odd red grouse or two if you're lucky. (Notices explain that despite this being Access Land paths across these moors may be closed for a few days during the grouse-shooting season, in which case retrace your steps to the Kinder valley.)

With the cabin on your right take the wide, sandy track to your left — not the one across the middle of the moor ahead. Before long go through a gate and fork left on a path across pasture, then follow this alongside a wall and through a succession of fields down the hillside towards Hayfield. On

your right you pass a fine stand of beech, the supposed 20 trees after which the cafe is named — but how many can you count?

This wide track, which connects with the Ashop valley on the far side of Kinder and is known as the Snake Path, finally drops down to a road by houses, where you should turn right and walk back into Hayfield. Approaching the main street turn left down the wide, cobbled alleyway opposite the grocers, then cross the bridge in front of the Royal Hotel and the cafe is on your left opposite the church. To return to the car park cross the road and cut through between the buildings opposite.

# Other titles from Dalesman

## *Dalesman Tea Shop Walks Series*
LAKE DISTRICT  Mary Welsh  5.99
YORKSHIRE DALES  Richard Musgrave  £5.99

## *Pub Walks Series*
LAKE DISTRICT  Terry Marsh  £5.99
LANCASHIRE  Terry Marsh  £5.99
NORTH YORK MOORS  & COAST  Richard Musgrave  £5.99
PEAK DISTRICT  John Morrison  £5.99
YORKSHIRE DALES  Richard Musgrave  £5.95

## *Walks Around Series*
BAKEWELL Martin Smith £1.99
BUXTON Andrew McCloy £1.99
CASTLETON John Gillham £1.99
MATLOCK Martin Smith £1.99
AMBLESIDE Tom Bowker £1.99
HAWKSHEAD Mary Welsh £1.99
KESWICK Dawn Gibson £1.99
WINDERMERE Robert Gambles £1.99
GRASSINGTON Richard Musgrave £1.99
SETTLE & MALHAM Richard Musgrave £1.99
HAWES Richard Musgrave £1.99
RICHMOND Richard Musgrave £1.99
PICKERING Nick Channer £1.99
WHITBY Nick Channer £1.99
KIRKBYMOORSIDE Nick Channer £1.99
HELMSLEY Nick Channer £1.99

Available from all good bookshops. In case of difficulty, and for a full list of
Dalesman titles,  contact Dalesman Publishing Company, Stable Courtyard,
Broughton Hall, Skipton, North Yorkshire,  BD23 3AZ. Tel: 01756 701381
web: http//www.dalesman.co.uk